MW00893171

FOUR LEGS
AND
A STRETCHER

To Annabelle —

All my best to you!

Rick

FOUR LEGS
AND
A STRETCHER

Constructing an Intentional Faith that Leads to Godliness

F. C. VOGT

Copyright © 2022 F. C. Vogt.

All rights reserved. No part of this book may be used or reproduced by any means, graphic, electronic, or mechanical, including photocopying, recording, taping or by any information storage retrieval system without the written permission of the author except in the case of brief quotations embodied in critical articles and reviews.

This book is a work of non-fiction. Unless otherwise noted, the author and the publisher make no explicit guarantees as to the accuracy of the information contained in this book and in some cases, names of people and places have been altered to protect their privacy.

Archway Publishing books may be ordered through booksellers or by contacting:

Archway Publishing
1663 Liberty Drive
Bloomington, IN 47403
www.archwaypublishing.com
844-669-3957

Because of the dynamic nature of the Internet, any web addresses or links contained in this book may have changed since publication and may no longer be valid. The views expressed in this work are solely those of the author and do not necessarily reflect the views of the publisher, and the publisher hereby disclaims any responsibility for them.

Any people depicted in stock imagery provided by Getty Images are models, and such images are being used for illustrative purposes only. Certain stock imagery © Getty Images.

Interior Image Credit: Nancy Beck

Scripture quotations are taken from The Holy Bible, New International Version®, NIV® Copyright © 1973, 1978, 1984, 2011 by Biblica, Inc.® Used by permission. All rights reserved worldwide.

ISBN: 978-1-6657-2705-1 (sc)
ISBN: 978-1-6657-2704-4 (hc)
ISBN: 978-1-6657-2706-8 (e)

Library of Congress Control Number: 2022913312

Print information available on the last page.

Archway Publishing rev. date: 9/22/2022

This book is dedicated to my wife, Patricia, and my daughter, Amelia. Without them, writing this book would not have been possible.

Contents

Part 3: Living Your Faith

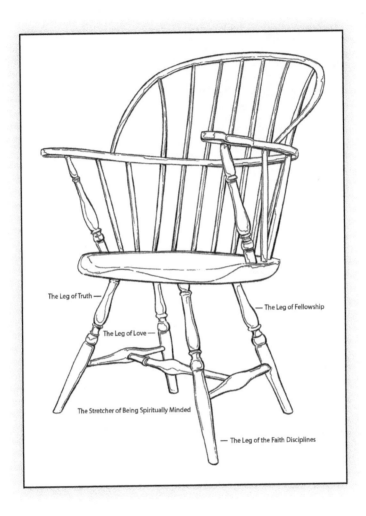

The Leg of Truth —

— The Leg of Fellowship

The Leg of Love —

The Stretcher of Being Spiritually Minded

— The Leg of the Faith Disciplines

Preface

A book is as dangerous as any journey you might take. The person who closes the back cover may not be the same one that opened the front one. Treat them with respect.[1]

The classic novel *The Agony and the Ecstasy*[2] was the starting point for my love of history. When I first read it at the age of fifteen, this biographical work describing the life of Michelangelo Buonarroti captured my attention like no other book I had read up to that point. At school, lessons about history were mechanical and boring. But this book introduced me to history as a story—a story about real people. Michelangelo's magnificent artistic creations became linchpins in time and a frame of reference for other historical events that piqued my interest. It made history real and meaningful to me.

I share this with you because it makes the point that we are intellectually and emotionally drawn to understand and conceptualize almost everything in different ways, and faith is no different. While the scriptures provide truth about what faith means, requires, and does, God created us as individuals, and the way we perceive and apply our faith is as varied as we are. As an artisan who makes and restores furniture, the metaphor of constructing our faith like the base of a chair speaks to me in a way that makes understanding faith plausible. For me, building a base of faith like a chair is an apt comparison with how we build the foundation for a spiritual, moral, and purposeful life. Perhaps this book's perspective will help make faith more real and practicable to you.

The five components of a chair base, that of four legs and a stretcher, represent five areas of spiritual formation that godly faith requires. The four legs symbolize truth, love, fellowship, and what I call the faith disciplines. The stretcher that connects them together characterizes the practice of being spiritually minded about them.

The author and designer of life intended for each of them to play a vibrant role in the way we construct our lives. Like a chair with a dependable base, a life supported by these five components can be secure, rewarding, and purposeful. We will study what comprises these elements of faith and how they are shaped. We will consider their interrelationship and connection with each other. We will examine how to build a base of godly faith that securely and dependably supports a fulfilling life.

We will also reflect on a lifelong journey as a metaphor for faith. While certainly not original to this book, this metaphor speaks to me as I recall my experiences on this path to God. It characterizes the direction and the purposeful steps we take to grow and mature in our faith and how we progress toward a life consecrated to God. It's a destination that I call the Promised Land of Godliness and define later in the book.

Yet, despite the anecdotes, metaphors, and personal experiences found here, this book is, at its core, a theological work. It is so because it is a study of the nature of God and religious belief. In his book *Everyone's a Theologian*, R. C. Sproul makes the point:

Many people believe that theological study holds little value. They say, "I don't need theology; I just need Jesus." Yet theology is unavoidable for every Christian. It is our attempt to understand the truth that God has revealed to us. So, it is not a question of whether we are going to engage in theology; it is a question of whether our theology is sound or unsound. It is important to study and learn because God has taken great pains to reveal Himself to His people. He gave us a book, one that is not meant to sit on a shelf pressing dried flowers but to be read, searched, digested, studied, and chiefly to be understood.[3]

God entrusted us with the responsibility to understand what He says in His Word, and He has given each of us the ability to do so. The purpose of theology is to bring us into the presence of the creator of the universe—God Almighty. It requires a studied and recurrent examination of the scriptures. However, even if our theology is sound and our understanding of the scriptures is patently accurate, a theology that is purely academic but that doesn't engage our hearts, provoke us to respond with passion and personal conviction, and, most importantly, bring us into a surrendered and loving relationship with our Lord is merely an intellectual and legalistic adherence to rules and regulations.

Faith is God's method for bringing humanity into consecrated fellowship with Him. Relative to this, faith is, at its core, about the presence of God in our lives. Faith determines the degree to which our knowledge *of God* develops into a relationship *with God*. Faith measures how we respond to that, deepen our understanding of it, and change our lives because of it.

The purpose of this book is primarily focused on building our understanding and practices of maturing in faith. Yet, despite all our efforts to grow in faith, there is an essential truth we must be constantly aware of: God has given us the capacity for faith in the first place. Without this, we would be incapable of faith, and our faith journey would be meaningless. When we genuinely began a spiritual journey in earnest, we were changed forever. We were given a new nature spiritually, which can understand spiritual truth, the godly purposes of life, and a heart that desires to please Him that was not there before.

The person without the Spirit does not accept the things that come from the Spirit of God but considers them foolishness and cannot understand them because they are discerned only through the Spirit. (1 Corinthians 2:14)

So as we work to build our faith and grow in spiritual formation, there is no place for pride or smugness. We would be incapable of spiritual growth if left on our own and without God's capabilities. The glory and honor of our faith belong to Him.

While this book is not a study of apologetics, it is written with some presumptions about reality and truth that are universally held by those who are followers of Jesus Christ:

God does, in fact, exist and desires a personal relationship with humankind.

There is such a thing as absolute truth.

The Bible reveals this truth, as it is the word of God.

Jesus is the son of God, the savior of humanity, and has invited all people to follow Him.

Jesus was crucified, died, and was raised from the dead to spiritually give us a new life.

We can live sanctified and holy lives.

Jesus wants His followers to fellowship together and help one another grow spiritually.

Jesus will return in the future to be with us eternally.

All people are made in God's image and are equally valuable to Him.

I understand and respect that these may not be current realities for you. But I would ask that you put your doubts and disagreements aside for a few hours and consider what is written here. There is no more important activity than determining what you believe and why when it comes to your spiritual life. If this book helps you do that in some way, it has served my purpose in writing it.

That being said, this book is *not* about:

followers of Jesus being more important to or loved by God more than others,

telling you that you need to join a church and go there every Sunday morning,

Christians being superior to everyone else and always right about everything,

or passing judgment on anyone who disagrees with what is written here.

If it were, I wouldn't want to read it either!

This book is about a relationship. It's about a relationship built upon unconditional love that needs no building to be genuine, has no pecking order of human value, and requires no comparison with or approval from others for validation.

God wants every part of us, but especially our hearts. And a heart-centered practice of building and growing in godly faith is what I hope to convey through the scriptures, some thoughts by other writers, some metaphors that have helped me, and some stories about the personal way God has been involved in drawing me to Him.

Faith from the heart is one that, while having its challenges, evokes a sense of peace and strength that cannot be found elsewhere.

Faith from the heart is sensitive to the needs of humankind and responds with the love and wisdom of God.

Faith from the heart is always thankful because it recognizes the blessings of God that might otherwise be overlooked.

Faith from the heart looks to God for answers that are difficult to come by and trusts God to provide.

The book *The Agony and the Ecstasy* gave me a fresh perspective of the relevance and importance of history. The quote by Mark Lawrence speaks to the power of words. I pray that the words on these pages will speak to your heart and have a helpful effect on your perspective and understanding of your faith journey.

List of abbreviations

AMP	Amplified Bible
CEV	Contemporary English Version
ESV	Eastern Standard Version
GWT	God's Word Translation
GNT	Good News Translation
KJV	King James Version
NET	NET Bible
NIV	New International Version
NLT	New Living Translation
Message	The Message Paraphrase

—— PART 1 ——

UNDERSTANDING YOUR FAITH

INTRODUCTION

Before you even had any inkling about the concept of faith, you had two things. You had life, and as part of that life, you had a mind that could think. As you grew older, you began to have thoughts that entertained what the meaning or purpose of your life was about. At that moment, you started a journey. It was a journey that was perhaps confusing or intimidating, inspiring or exciting, full of wonder and imagination, seemingly impossible and without hope, or even short-lived and abandoned. But the critical point here is that your journey, no matter how it has played out thus far, began with the way you think. This first section—"Understanding Your Faith"—will challenge how you think about your faith and hopefully inspire and energize you to pursue it more intentionally.

CHAPTER 1

CHANGING DIRECTION

Nothing whatever, whether great or small, can happen to a believer, without God's ordering and permission. There is no such thing as "chance," "luck," or "accident" in the Christian's journey through this world. All is arranged and appointed by God. And all things are "working together" for the believer's good.

—*J. C. Ryle*

On a warm summer morning in July of 1971, I was making a trip to northern New Mexico to visit some friends who lived on a well-known commune of hippies. I admired them and considered them to be very spiritual people. I was curious about how they had arrived at this place of what appeared to me as genuine spirituality. They epitomized the popular anthem of the day, "tune in, turn on, drop out," and I was hopeful that if I could experience some time with them in their isolated and "holy" environment, I too would come to understand what spiritual life was all about. I was eighteen years old, and I wanted what they had.

Spirituality was of great interest to me, yet any meaningful sense of it had eluded me. While I had very kind and loving parents, I had little exposure to a spiritual life growing up. We frequently went to different churches on Sundays, but the worship and teachings seemed rigid, judgmental, and superficial. And outside of Sunday worship, so many people that called themselves Christians seemed no different than anyone else. They never talked about the spiritual aspects of life. They drank too much, lost their tempers, their language could be mean and foul, gossiped about each other, had affairs, and divorced. Their primary focus seemed to be on making money.

In contrast, my non-Christian hippie friends seemed genuinely kind, content, peaceful, and not ensnared with the unrestrained materialism I grew up around. Their beliefs were visibly evident in their demeanor, behavior, and lifestyle. And especially, they seemed to know a lot about spirituality.

Three days into my trip, I was sitting beside my motorcycle at a rest stop in central Kansas, taking a break from the three hours of driving I had just completed. As I was sitting there, a man in a pickup truck with a cap on the back pulled in, and his family of five headed into the restrooms. As the man exited the restroom, he noticed me sitting next to my bike and came over and struck up a conversation while he waited for the rest of his family.

During the conversation, I noticed that the difference in our appearance could not have been more striking. He was clean-shaven, had a buzz haircut, and was neatly and conservatively dressed, with beautiful and highly polished cowboy boots. I was dressed in the typical hippie garb of the day with very long hair and an earring. He was about twenty years older than me.

I told him I was traveling from Cincinnati to northern New Mexico for a couple of weeks and enjoyed motorcycle travel. He complimented me on my choice of motorcycles and began to reminisce of his younger, more carefree days of similar bike trips all over the West. He explained that he and his family were headed to a rodeo a few towns away.

He asked me why I was traveling to northern New Mexico, as it was such a long trip from Cincinnati. With great pride and a sense of superiority, I told him that I was going there to find God. He quietly looked down at the ground for a moment, and when he raised his head and looked me in the eye, he said he was sorry to hear that.

I was somewhat taken aback by what he said. I asked him why he could be sorry to hear what I smugly thought was a unique and even erudite answer to his question. He then made a statement that caused me to change the direction of my life that continues to this day.

He said that he was sorry that my God was so small that I had to drive all the way to New Mexico to be with Him and that his God was everywhere and with him wherever he was.

That statement affected me so deeply because I knew what he said had to be true in my heart. I certainly wanted it to be true. From my earliest memories, I knew there was a personal God, and I genuinely wanted to know Him and be convinced that He knew and cared for me. I wanted to be close to Him, yet I felt like an outsider when it came to God. Over the brief span of my life, that kind of personal relationship with God seemed out of grasp.

For the next few minutes, he went on to talk to me about the word of God—the scriptures—and how they revealed God. He spoke of Jesus Christ and how He could lead me into a personal and intimate relationship with the true God and that this God would never leave or forsake me but always be with me. He said that I should ask myself not only if God was with me, but was I with God?

We parted ways, and I continued my trip to the commune in New Mexico. Spending time with my friends proved to be a disappointment. I discovered that the spiritual qualities I perceived they had were just as superficial as those I had experienced growing up. They depended on mind-altering drugs to achieve a connection with God. This didn't make sense to me because I didn't need drugs to have a relationship with people, so why would they be needed for a relationship with God Almighty? They, too, lost their tempers and said hurtful things to each other. They were just as judgmental toward those who were different than them. My time there opened my eyes to the fact that the spiritual path I was on was a journey to nowhere. So, I cut my trip short and headed home with excitement and enthusiasm for embarking on my spiritual journey in a new way, with different directions, and a new vision of what my spiritual life could possibly look like.

I share this story with you because it illustrates something required of each of us and will continue throughout our lives as we embark on a journey of faith. It has to do with the way we think. What caused me to change my spiritual direction initially was not a feeling, not a sign, not a vision, not a revelation. It began with changing the way *I thought about* the direction of my life and the destination I was headed toward. Something about what was said caused me to reconsider what I believed to be true.

Knowing what we believe and why we believe it is one of the most significant aspects of a purposeful life. It's a process that should continue throughout our lives.

The highly regarded theologian R. C. Sproul made a yearly habit of writing down his ten most important beliefs and why he believed them.[1] He would then evaluate these beliefs using three criteria: the infallibility of the source of his beliefs, his ability to articulate why he believed what he did, and the strength of his conviction to those beliefs. If he determined that his beliefs failed to meet any of these criteria, he would address the cause and make changes as needed. I'll ask you a challenging question that I often ask myself. How would your core values and beliefs hold up under this scrutiny?

If we get on our bathroom scale in the morning and find that our weight is not what it should be, we choose what we are going to do with that information. On the one hand, we may decide to do nothing because we're not concerned about the consequences. On the other, we may decide to make some changes in our behavior because our weight is headed in a direction we don't care for! Spiritual self-examination is like getting on that scale. It's a spiritual "weigh-in."

Do you need to spend some time on that scale?

Self-examination is a spiritually necessary and healthy exercise when practiced in a godly way. God has given each of us this responsibility, and scripture says much about it.

> But test everything; hold fast what is good. (1 Thessalonians 5:21 ESV)

> When I think on my ways, I turn my feet to your testimonies. (Psalm 119:59 ESV)

> In all your ways, acknowledge him, and he will make straight your paths. (Proverbs 3:6 ESV)

Men and women of faith must be men and women of thought. This is not to say that the process of maturing in our faith is purely a mental exercise. Knowledge alone isn't going to change anything. But it is where we begin.

I encourage you to spend time in honest and humble personal introspection. Don't spend it alone; spend it with God. It could be daily, early each morning, or once a week for a few weeks. Or you might elect to go away somewhere for an extended period. (Chapter 11 and appendix 2 take a deep dive into this.) What is important is that you take the necessary time to effectively evaluate and understand the condition of your faith and where you are headed with it.

Apostle Peter's first charge in his sermon to the church on the day of Pentecost was to repent—to change their minds and hearts and turn their focus from the truth as they perceived it to the truth that Jesus personified.

When the people heard this, they were cut to
the heart and asked Peter and the other apostles,
"Brothers, what shall we do?" Peter replied, "Repent
and be baptized, every one of you, in the name of
Jesus Christ for the forgiveness of your sins, and
you will receive the gift of the Holy Spirit." (Acts
2:37–38)

The reality communicated here is that if you want to turn the
direction of your life to point toward God, if you're going to arrive
at a place of genuine spiritual faith, the *first* thing you need to do
is to change the way you think! Would we all value and take this
charge to change direction to heart. This is the first requirement of
our journey to the Promised Land of Godliness.

Watch your thoughts, they become your words; watch your words,
they become your actions; watch your actions, they become your
habits; watch your habits, they become your character; watch your
character, it becomes your destiny.

As this insightful twenty-five-hundred-year-old saying so
eloquently states, our thoughts are the starting point for what we
do with our lives and eventually become.[2] But while our thoughts
are the starting point for our faith, it doesn't end there. In the
following chapters, we will build on this starting point and define
what composes genuine faith and what it looks like in practice.

If you take only one thing away from this chapter, I entreat
you to take this: the direction of our journey of faith begins and
continues based on how we think. The King James Version famously
translates Proverbs 23:7: "as he thinks in his heart, so is he."

What do your thoughts about God tell you about the direction
of your faith?

CHAPTER 2

THE PROMISED LAND
OF GODLINESS

---

*The Christian experience, from start to finish, is a
journey of faith.*

—*Watchman Nee*

Perhaps the most remarkable mass journey ever undertaken in human
history was that of Israel's Exodus from slavery in Egypt to freedom
in the promised land of Canaan. The books of Exodus through
Deuteronomy record this story. A striking aspect of this record is
the amount of time and information devoted to documenting the
events, victories, and setbacks over these forty years.

The narrative of this epic journey encompasses about 10 percent
of the Old Testament. More is written about it than all the gospels
combined, all the church epistles, and apostle Paul's missionary
journeys. The volume of information that the scriptures devote to
this journey speaks to its importance and should arouse our interest.
There is much to learn from this event.

A powerful lesson in this record stands out as particularly
relevant to our own journey of maturing in faith. It involves an

issue that surfaces numerous times and applies to us. It is revealed by answering one question: Why did a journey of fewer than two hundred miles, which could have been made in a few months or less, take forty years?

Jesus walked a little over three thousand miles during His three years of ministry. Apostle Paul traveled approximately ten thousand miles over nine years, including lengthy stays in many cities and towns. The disparity in time and distance when comparing these travel histories with Israel's is striking. The discrepancy between the living conditions in Egypt and those anticipated in the Promised Land should have motivated Israel to arrive there as quickly as possible. So, why did the trip take approximately 160 times longer than it could have?

Such a long journey was not the primary will of God. Even a cursory read of the Exodus record makes this very clear. This is evidenced by the fact that God provided them with "a pillar of cloud to guide them on their way and by night in a pillar of fire to give them light so that they could travel by day or night."[1] Additionally, He kept them fed, healthy and protected from enemies so they could arrive in Canaan safely and quickly.

The record clarifies that the ultimate cause of so many delays lies solely at the feet of Israel. Despite all the miraculous ways that God provided for them, protected them, and undeniably proved His presence with them, they were constantly drawn to the false sense of security and provision of being enslaved people in Egypt. They doubted the freedom and abundance that God promised them upon their arrival in Canaan. They allowed their hard-hearted, fearful, and unbelieving attitudes toward God to govern their behavior. This attitude resulted in disobedience and rebellion toward the truth of what God had promised. The bottom line is that they consistently refused to have faith in God to guide and give purpose to their journey. Because of this, the Promised Land and its blessings became an overly optimistic and unreachable destination to them.

As a result, the Israelites suffered the consequences of their unbelief. Except for Joshua and Caleb, none of the million-plus people of their generation made it into the Promised Land.

In the context of the point made in the last chapter—that the direction of our journey of faith is initially based on how we think—let's reflect on what we can learn from Israel's journey to the Promised Land through five considerations.

CONSIDER WHAT GOVERNS YOUR DECISIONS

We can look at the plight of Israel during the Exodus and ask, how could they possibly not trust God to do what He said He would do—bring them safely into the promised land—after the miracles and deliverance they had seen with their own eyes? How could they question His love for them and faithfulness to keep His covenants? What was the driving force that caused them to change the way they thought about the promises of God?

The relevance of this record to us today becomes clear when we ask ourselves, are we really that different from Israel?

Despite all that God has done and does for us daily, How often has our progress of maturity in knowing, loving, and trusting God turned into a lengthy and arduous journey because of our ignorance, fear, and self-willed rebelliousness toward God?

Does the power and influence of our past frequently sidetrack or hinder us from growing in faith?

Does arriving at a place of confidence in the love, mercy, grace, and forgiveness that God has lavished on us in Christ appear as an elusive and unreachable reality?

Aren't we just as fearful, rebellious, hard-hearted, and doubtful as Israel was too often?

I can ask these questions without hubris because I have experienced and battled with all of this! I know what God has brought me out of, and I still fail to have faith in Him sometimes. I am "in the camp" just like Israel was. I study, I pray, I work, I attend the meetings and the fellowships. I volunteer, I serve, I teach, and I give. It seems like I have all the knowledge of the truth I need but too often fail to practice what I know. I get sidetracked from moving in an intentional direction and with measurable progress toward maturing in faith. I want to rationalize and blame my upbringing, "genetic makeup," culture, wife, church, parents, life circumstances, weakness of character, busy schedule, and even Adam and Eve!

But in my heart, I know these aren't the reasons I'm not always where God wants me to be spiritually. And in those contemplative moments of quiet honesty and reflection, I know the real cause is that I can be just like Israel—mired in a spiritual malaise and apathy and self-absorbed with my own needs. I get paralyzed by my immaturity, fear of failure, and unbelief. I can allow my self-talk to question, "Is this as good as my faith gets?" As a dear friend of mine often asks when he is preaching, "Am I walking down your street?"

Maybe you can relate to apostle Paul as he wrestled with what governed his decisions. The Message version of Romans 7:14–24 puts it into words that speak loudly to me:

> I know that all God's commands are spiritual, but I'm not. Isn't this also your experience? Yes. I'm full of myself; after all, I've spent a long time in sin's prison. What I don't understand about myself is that I decide one way, but then I act another, doing things I absolutely despise. So, if I can't be trusted to figure out what is best for myself and then do it, it becomes obvious that God's command is necessary.

But I need something *more*! For if I know the law but still can't keep it, and if the power of sin within me keeps sabotaging my best intentions, I obviously need help! I realize that I don't have what it takes. I can will it, but I can't *do* it. I decide to do good, but I don't *really* do it; I decide not to do bad, but then I do it anyway. My decisions, such as they are, don't result in actions. Something has gone wrong deep within me and gets the better of me every time.

It happens so regularly that it's predictable. The moment I decide to do good, sin is there to trip me up. I truly delight in God's commands, but it's pretty obvious that not all of me joins in that delight. Parts of me covertly rebel, and just when I least expect it, they take charge. I've tried everything, and nothing helps. I'm at the end of my rope. Is there no one who can do anything for me? Isn't that the real question?

When Paul exclaimed, "I'm at the end of my rope. Is there no one who can do anything for me?" we find he provides the answer in the next verse.

> The answer, thank God, is that Jesus Christ can and does. He acted to set things right in this life of contradictions where I want to serve God with all my heart and mind, but am pulled by the influence of sin to do something totally different. (Romans 7:25)

Unpacking this answer and how to live it speaks to the focal point of what is the driving force in our lives. We all have motivations, reasons, values, and priorities that govern our decisions. Too often, these priorities are driven by the values of the me-first culture we live in, such as the need for acceptance and recognition, unbridled materialism, instant gratification, and avoiding accountability for our bad choices. But in view of living a godly life, what *should* they be?

Most churches and businesses have what is called a "mission statement." This is usually a brief definition that succinctly defines the primary reason for their existence, their singularly most important goal, and the purpose behind everything they do. How would it read if you were to write a one-sentence "mission statement" for your life? Do you allow it to govern the decisions you make?

CONSIDER YOUR DESTINATION

Because we are on a journey of faith and spirituality, our mission statement needs to include a destination. What, then, is our destination? I call it the Promised Land of Godliness. I define godliness as a deeply intimate and consecrated relationship with Almighty God that dominates and governs every aspect of how we live.

The Promised Land of Godliness is used as a metaphor for the destination of our journey of faith, compared to the journey of Israel from Egypt to the Promised Land of Canaan. Godliness is not a spiritual or emotional state of nirvana, enlightenment, or transcendental bliss. Nor is it a physical Shangri-La, paradise, or heaven on earth. Like Canaan, it is not necessarily a place without conflict, pain, or suffering. Those ordeals will be with us until the return of Christ and the establishment of the new heavens and earth. In the New Testament, God calls us to a place of genuine spirituality that fosters a fruitful new life of grace, peace, joy, contentment, purpose, hope, and strength. It is a spiritual rather than physical destination. It is a destination that God wills for everyone and is available to all who will deliberately follow His directions.

It's a place of intimate and purposeful fellowship with the creator of the universe.

It's a place where, despite all our imperfections, faults, failures, and weaknesses, we can stand before Almighty God, wholly convinced of His forgiveness and unconditional love and acceptance by Him.

It's a place of strength, confidence, and freedom because we are devoted to His way, surrendered to His truth, and blessed with the abundant life that He provides.

It's a lifestyle that reflects being fully and wholly consecrated to God.

Ralph Waldo Emerson is famously quoted in his book *Self Reliance*: "Life is a journey, not a destination"[2] He is making the point that life is to be lived fully, and the daily blessings of it are to be observed, enjoyed, and appreciated. I think we would all agree with this, but at the same time, a journey without a destination is kind of pointless. The relevant significance of the destination makes any journey worthwhile and intentional. It brings purpose, vitality, value, and meaning to the journey.

Likewise, a life with no meaningful purpose or destination is pointless. A life with no significant purpose or destination devolves into a short-term quest for immediate gratification, emotional or intellectual entertainment, and self-serving values and activities. It has no vision beyond the foreseeable future. It does not concern itself with legacy, heritage, helping meet the needs of humankind or personal future consequence. So, I believe that it is accurate to say that a fulfilling life is an intentional journey *with* an essential destination.

The destination I call the Promised Land of Godliness.

CONSIDER YOUR DIRECTIONS

Much of the record of the Exodus could be compared to the journey that God is inviting us on today. It's not without challenges. Israel's travails on the way to the Promised Land illustrate the pitfalls we face. We are tempted to turn from God's path for internal and external reasons, many of which will be examined in this book. And, just like Israel, the "Egypt call" of our secular culture offers a perceived sense of truth that appears to offer security, ease, comfort, and acceptance. This appeals to our human nature, even though its destination is a return to a type of mental, moral, and spiritual slavery. We are cautioned of this in Proverbs: "There is a way that appears to be right, but in the end it leads to death" (Proverbs16:25).

In our me-first culture that exalts relative truth, many ways appear correct, yet they can wind up being a dead-end street. The signs alerting us of our bad choices can be unrecognizable if they are overgrown with weeds of bad information and self-centered motivations. We can become convinced that we are making the right decision, yet we wind up in the wrong place. Sometimes it can be difficult or seemingly impossible to turn around.

In stark contrast, God's directions lead us on a journey of ever-increasing grace, peace, joy, contentment, hope, strength, and purpose.

> You have made known to me the path of life. (Psalm 16:11)

Our loving God not only provides us with a way out of our dead ends, but He also imparts to us directions that intentionally and measurably move us in the direction of true faith and godliness.

Every purposeful journey needs directions on how to arrive at its destination. All of us have experienced the frustration of incorrect or misleading directions that make a trip much more difficult and lengthier than it could have been. Too often, we can make the common mistake of thinking that our desire or passion for maturing in faith is all that is required. However, in what pastor Andy Stanley calls the "Principle of the Path," he states that "our directions, not our intentions, determine our destination."[3] The point is that it is not how much we desire to arrive at a particular place, or how noble or selfless our motives are that brings us to our destination. It is following the directions during our journey that will get us there. Consequently, the directions we have must be accurate and true.

The directions are called faith.

CONSIDER THE HEART OF THE MATTER

What we are really talking about here is transformation.

I believe that everyone wants a meaningful, purposeful, and fulfilling life. Every person has an innate desire to accomplish something special, something valuable, and something unique to them. The accomplishment of these longings is often buried or veiled by a self-image and value system that has been sabotaged and redirected away from what God has called us to be. The reasons for this are many and often valid, and we will delve into many of them. The good news is that they can be overcome by God's transformative truth, power, and intentional involvement in our lives.

God has made every person in His image and values every life. We need not be bound to explanations of what God can and cannot do by those that do not know Him or what He is capable of, no matter their credentials and notoriety, or as erudite as they appear to be. Neither can we rely on the government's abilities, political ideologies, social programs, or secular educational systems to provide us with remedies for the transformation of the human heart. The truth of God's capabilities has been made known to us by a far more consistently dependable source—God Himself.

> Now to him who is able to do immeasurably more than all we ask or imagine, according to his power that is at work within us, to him be glory in the church and in Christ Jesus throughout all generations, for ever and ever! Amen. (Ephesians 3:20)

Scriptures are very clear as to what is involved and required of us for spiritual transformation to occur. But we are not capable of this alone. It is God's truth, love, and power at work in our lives that brings this about.

> Now the Lord is the Spirit, and where the Spirit of the Lord is, there is freedom. And we all, who with unveiled faces contemplate the Lord's glory, are being transformed into his image with ever-increasing glory, which comes from the Lord, who is the Spirit. (2 Corinthians 3:17–18)

Israel's extended wanderings in the wilderness, rather than a direct route taking them to where God wanted them to be, was primarily due to a heart problem. It took a generation to change that. But it doesn't have to become the story of our faith journey.

Personal transformation into a life defined by godliness is the purpose of the journey and the heart of the matter.

On our journey to the Promised Land of Godliness, God has not left us alone, unequipped, or impotent. He has provided us with the directions and ability to intentionally and measurably experience His purposes for our lives. God never intended for His people, His children, or His family to feel isolated or distant from Him, powerless over the challenges of life that this fallen world can confront us with or bereft of meaning and purpose.

All of us are going somewhere. If Galatians 6:7 is true, that we reap what we sow, then the directions we sow in this life, if accurate, dependable, practical, and done with intention, will eventually bring us to the destination they point us toward. How would your life change, and what would it look like if you were to follow the trustworthy directions to the destination that God has called you to?

No matter your location on this journey, no matter the degree of godly transformation you aspire to or have experienced, I want to ask you a question that forms an important point to consider from this chapter. Some will know the answer immediately; some will be unsure about it, while others may have never considered it. It's a question that we probably should ask ourselves frequently throughout our lives: Is what you believe, value, and trust pointing you toward Egypt or Canaan?

CHAPTER 3

THE PICTURE OF FAITH

To one who has faith, no explanation is necessary.
To one without faith, no explanation is possible.
—*Thomas Aquinas*

If you asked someone what the 1,225-page novel *War and Peace* was about, and they replied, "Well, Napoleon lost," that answer would be accurate but far from complete. While correct about that one point, it would hardly convey the military history, political upheaval, and cultural drama of the fifteen years it chronicles about the French invasion of Russia during the French Revolution and the impact of the Napoleonic era on Tsarist society and beyond. The book is structured to comprehensively present the entire story with great detail.[1]

Similarly, as described in the Bible, faith has a comprehensive narrative that must be understood if it is to be lived out in the way that God intended it. Faith cannot be defined by one verse or one sentence. Like the simplistic description of *War and Peace*, doing so devalues its meaning and purpose, resulting in an inadequate picture of genuine faith.

Godly faith forms the basis of our relationship with God, is at the core of our self-identity, and defines how we live. It provides the context for our spiritual formation and growth. It is our most valued Christlike quality. Considering the enormity of faith's significance to our lives, we need to clearly understand it.

In the next chapter, we will look at five major components that make up what I call the structure of faith and how we can use this structure to live out our faith beliefs in a way that deepens our relationship with God and impacts the world in a way that honors God. Before we do, I want to make sure we are on the same page regarding the definition of faith. I want to clarify some of the fundamental truths about it and examine some of the mistaken notions. I'm not breaking any new theological ground here. I'm attempting to recultivate some "old ground" of understanding and practice that people who spoke the Bible's language knew very well. It is an understanding that has been diminished over the centuries, and even more so over the last century.

THE BASIC PICTURE

Part of the cause of misunderstanding biblical faith has been its movement away from the word's initial meaning, which simply means trust, confidence, and assurance. Trust is defined as a firm belief in the character, strength, or truth of someone or something. It results from the dependability, reliability, and consistent trustworthiness of what or whom we are to have trust in. This can be confirmed by reading any reliable Bible dictionary or lexicon. The Revised English Version helps to clarify this because it reads "trust," where almost all other versions read "faith."

No matter which version of the New Testament you read, the words faith, assurance, trust, and believe are almost always translated from the same Greek root word and can frequently be used interchangeably, depending on the context.

THE BIG PICTURE

While it is important to understand the word itself, simply defining faith based on a study of its etymology alone fails to convey the depth, influence, and impact of what it means to live by faith. That's because trust is more than a word. The practice of faith, or trusting God, can be defined as living out what we believe He says is true. It always includes corresponding behavior. It is both a verb and a noun. Scriptures make the point that faith that does nothing is useless. And when we dig into the Bible to learn about faith as God characterizes it, we find that faith is comprehensive and richly defined. A simple review of what the Bible says about faith reveals:

We are saved and receive eternal life through faith.

We are justified by faith.

We are sanctified by faith.

We are made righteous by faith.

We please God by faith.

We stand, walk, and live by faith.

Faith makes us whole.

Faith is the assurance of what we hope for and the certainty of what we do not see.

Christ dwells in our hearts by faith.

Our hearts are purified by faith.

Prayers are answered by faith.

Faith is the way we enter God's will for our lives.

With these scriptural components of faith in mind, various Christian writers have provided insightful descriptions of it:

Faith is the basic ingredient to begin a relationship with God.

It is wholly trusting and relying upon Him for all things. It is not just mental assent to the facts and realities of truth—it must come from a deep inner conviction.

It is the act whereby a person lays hold of God's resources, becomes obedient to what He has prescribed, and, putting aside all self-interest and self-reliance, trusts Him completely.

Faith is confidence in what we hope for and the assurance that the Lord is working no matter the situation, even though we cannot see it.

It is an unqualified surrender of the whole of one's being in dependence upon Him.

Faith is the connecting power into the spiritual realm, which links us with God and makes Him become a tangible reality to a person's sense perceptions.

From these descriptions of faith, it becomes evident that there is one fundamental and truth about faith woven into every aspect of its meaning: genuine faith is always inextricably connected to an intentional, trusting, and worshipful relationship with God.

Secularly, faith is often used synonymously with hope or trust in something *other than* God. We have all heard and possibly used the phrases have faith in yourself have faith in the system, have faith in humanity, etc. But when it comes to the faith of God, the accurate knowledge of it cannot be separated from God.

For our knowledge of faith to become meaningful and reflect the faith of Jesus Christ, we must yearn for it to define who we are. It requires a deep love for God and humble submission to living in a way that is surrendered to trusting His will over ours, being confident in what He says is available from Him, and being assured of His ability to provide it.

THE BLANK PICTURE

Perhaps one of the ways to validate the importance of faith is to consider the consequences of living without it.

Without faith, the meaning and purpose of your life would be based on your culture's superficial and self-centered values. Godly faith provides the highest values, selfless character, genuine integrity, and purest motives for a meaningful life.

Without faith, the scriptures become just words on a page. The reason they have significance is because of your faith.

Without faith, you would have no hope in this life and beyond. You have hope because of your faith.

Without faith, your prayers would be words expressed without confidence or anticipation of their being heard, much less answered. Your prayers are meaningful and powerful because of your faith.

Without faith, you would not have a personal or meaningful relationship with God and Jesus Christ. These relationships are built upon faith.

Faith brings you into the right relationship with Him.

The blank picture of a life without faith is one with no context or purpose outside of oneself.

THE FAKE PICTURE

I once received a photo postcard from a friend fishing for brown trout in Wyoming. In the picture, my friend was standing beside the Snake River, dressed in his fly-fishing garb and holding what he considered his prize catch. What stood out was that he was not carrying a fish but an eight-foot-long alligator! Obviously, the photo had been altered to be funny, but it looked real. With the technology available today, photographs can be altered so that almost any impossible scenario appears to be genuine.

I think the picture of faith has been altered in such a way. It has all too frequently devolved into an esoteric mixture of bad theology, popular psychology, and magical thinking. These are strong words but nonetheless justified as we will see in the following commonly believed fallacies about faith: faith is not an excuse for ignorance.

This lack of knowledge is demonstrated by the expression, "take it on faith." This phrase is most often used when someone can't explain something in the scriptures. While this has been considered a scriptural truth for centuries, it never occurs in the Bible, and is not a biblical concept. The confusion is partly due to not understanding the difference between acceptance and trust. People who are unsure of what faith means consent to the teaching that they can trust in something they don't understand. We can "accept" something even if we don't understand it, but "accepting" something is not "trust."

God did not create us to make ourselves trust something untrustworthy. God did not create us to believe in something for which there is no evidence of its existence! God expects us to educate ourselves in the truth He provides in scripture. That's why He provided it!

The most significant consequence of scriptural ignorance is falling prey to deceptive theologies. They usually come in the form of a type of sophistry that sounds plausible, maybe even makes sense, but it's not true! And the most effective kind of deception is to convince people that they are right when they are wrong. When we become comfortable with error, including error in our spiritual beliefs, we don't question its validity. If we think that we are facing the truth of God when we are instead turned away from it, we have been successfully deceived.

If my six-year-old granddaughter had looked at the photo of my friend catching an alligator from the Snake River in Wyoming, she would have considered it real. She would not have had enough knowledge to understand the impossibility of that. We can be like that in our understanding of the truth of scriptures, and result is that we are misled into thinking that the picture of faith we hold in our minds is accurate when it is not.

And one of the most pervasive deceptions that present a fake picture of faith is the second fallacy about it: faith is not a force that makes something happen.

The teaching that faith is a force portends that what happens in our life is directly proportional to the degree of the power of our thoughts. Faith, or "believing" as it is sometimes called, has no power in and of itself. It is not some metaphysical ability of the mind that gets you what you want. This is an idea that has been promulgated by spiritualists, self-help gurus, and evangelical ministers over the last century and a half. It was born out of the Divine Science and New Thought spiritualist movements.[2] It falsely promotes that *we* are in control of the cause or power behind something, rather than *trusting in* the cause of power. When scriptures say that things happen "by" or "through" faith, they don't mean that our faith is the cause but that our faith points to or trusts in the cause.

The error of this belief can easily be deconstructed. For instance, we trust or have faith that we will get our paycheck each week, but that does not make our employer write the check. We trust or have faith that our flight will leave on time, but that isn't what gets the plane off the ground. We trust or have faith that the medicine we are taking will remove our pain, but that does not cause the chemical reactions that make it work. This point is made even more apparent when you consider that you may *not* believe these things will happen, and they still will!

If we approach life with a viewpoint that faith in the abilities of our mind and thinking process somehow has the power to achieve anything, there would be no need for God in our lives. We could accomplish everything on our own and by our own power. The life, death, and resurrection of Jesus Christ would be of no value. We can't command God around by our faith, as if God is obligated to obey our orders. God is sovereign! The deceptive and dangerous message of this erroneous understanding of faith is that we are in charge of the will of God. That's called idolatry.

One more fake picture of faith must be corrected: faith is not the absence of doubt.

I can speak to this, as I was a member of a church that promoted all forms of doubt as sin with great conviction. I became afraid of doubt. I was scared that it would bring the power and grace of God at work in my life to a halt. I was afraid that it would invalidate my faith. I considered it to be a sin. As I have continued my faith journey, I've learned that doubts are more like rocks or roots along our path that we need to learn how to step over or go around. They might slow us down for a while or cause us to pause, but they don't have to stop us. This line of reasoning is poignantly made by Greg Laurie, a pastor at Harvest Christian Fellowship: "It is not necessarily bad to have moments of doubt. Sometimes we need to go through the foyer of doubt to get to the sanctuary of certainty."[3]

When it comes to trusting God, doubt has some understandable causes when:

Our issues or problems seem overwhelming.

We can't see how the situation will be settled.

The promises of God seem too good to be true.

Our prayers are taking a while to be answered.

We have failed, especially over a long time, to overcome things from our past.

We don't know why God allows this circumstance or why God acts as He does.

I have gone through these seasons of doubt, and they continue to arise from time to time. But I have become convinced that faith can live and even flourish with unanswered questions and that doubt is simply faith *with* questions.

This is not to say that doubt is a desirable frame of mind for your relationship with God! But it doesn't mean that you don't love God, aren't committed to be consecrated to being obedient to Him, or are outside of fellowship with God. But for maturing on your journey of faith and getting to the place God wants you to be, you must endeavor to resolve the issues that are causing your doubts to arise.

I'd like to offer some perspectives that have helped me work through seasons of doubt and overcome them.

First, doubt is not unbelief. As I said previously, I used to be afraid of doubt. The root of this fear was equating doubt with unbelief. Doubt and unbelief have very different meanings, and they are not synonyms. They are translated from entirely different Greek words. Doubt involves hesitation and indecision about what we believe, what we're being told, or are seeing. Unbelief conveys the meaning of distrust and disobedience. Doubt is an unsettled state of opinion concerning the reality of an event. Unbelief is refusing to believe that the event ever happened. Doubt is questioning what you believe. Unbelief is a determined refusal to believe.

Doubt can be healthy when it causes us to examine and understand the truth. As stated by Os Guinness:

> If ours is an examined faith, we should be unafraid to doubt. If doubt is eventually justified, we were believing what clearly was not worth believing. But if doubt is answered, our faith has grown stronger. It knows God more certainly, and it can enjoy God more deeply.[4]

The twentieth chapter of John's gospel tells us that Thomas was one of the twelve disciples of Jesus. He loved Jesus, and his description as a disciple speaks to the genuineness of his faith. But Thomas was not present when Jesus appeared to the other disciples, soon after His resurrection. Jesus showed the other disciples His hands and side. They were overjoyed at what they had seen. But when they later told Thomas that Jesus had been resurrected from the dead, he doubted what they were saying. He wanted to see the same proof that Jesus showed them. When Jesus eventually appeared to Thomas, he provided that same proof, and Thomas's doubts were removed entirely. He then joyfully exclaimed, "My Lord and my God!"[5]

Thomas was a real person, just like you and me. Put yourself in Thomas's shoes in this story. Let's say that William, the preacher at your church, suffers a horrible death. You attend the funeral and see him buried at the interment. You mourn his passing because he was near and dear to you. A few days later, your close friends tell you that William is no longer dead, has gotten out of his coffin, dug his way out of the ground, and is walking around visiting people. You tell them, "Yeah, right. I'll believe that when I see it." A little over a week later, you're with the same friends watching the evening news, and William appears in the room out of thin air and says, "Peace be with you!"

When you consider what Thomas doubted, that a dead person buried for three days was now alive again, you can probably relate to his hesitation. What would your response be? Might you think, *I can't believe what I'm seeing?* Would you need a little more convincing that what you're seeing is real? Might you totally freak out, call the police, and run for your life? I'm pretty sure I would.

There is a lesson about doubt in this record that helps put it in perspective and that shows us how to overcome it. We tend to focus on Thomas's doubt as a bad thing and leave it there. But we need to look further and see the picture that Thomas provides of how to overcome doubt. We call him "doubting Thomas" when he should be called "how to overcome doubt Thomas." Thomas was not complacent about his doubt, nor did he allow it to cause him to walk away from Jesus or His followers. Instead, he pursued the cause of his doubt. He needed more information, more facts, and more understanding to believe and trust that Jesus was who He said He was. He humbly and honestly faced his hesitation with believing and confessed his need to his fellow disciples, and God provided the answer that removed his doubt. Once he overcame his doubt, his faith was stronger for it.

God does not want or expect you to live with doubt. He knows you inside and out. He knows what is easy for you to believe and what is not. He does not condemn you for having it, but He definitely wants you to overcome it. Doubt is not sinning, but it can entice you into unbelief, which is. What is important is how we *respond* to doubt. It's OK to question what we don't understand, seek answers to circumstances that make us wonder if God is involved, and confess our confusion over unresolved problems to Him. These seasons of doubt do not invalidate our faith. They are opportunities to learn how to have faith.

If you need wisdom, ask our generous God, and He will give it to you. He will not rebuke you for asking. But when you ask him, be sure that your faith is in God alone. Do not waver, for a person with divided loyalty is as unsettled as a wave of the sea that is blown and tossed by the wind. Such people should not expect to receive anything from the Lord. Their loyalty is divided between God and the world, and they are unstable in everything they do (James 1:5–8 NLT).

John the Baptist, Gideon, Moses, Zacharias and Elizabeth, Abraham and Sarah, and even those charged by Jesus Himself with the great commission recorded in Matthew 28 all went through seasons of doubt and yet had genuine faith. They were real people with challenges, successes, failures, doubts, and hesitation, just like you and me. I encourage you to study their lives and see *how* they overcame doubt. Fill your mind with the truth of God's word concerning any doubts you have; seek out a trusted friend for godly counsel, and humbly and honestly lay the doubts before God and ask for His help. Your resolved doubts will cause your faith to flourish.

> So then, be very careful how you live. Don't live like foolish people but wise people. Make the most of your opportunities because these are evil days. So don't be foolish, but understand what the Lord wants. (Ephesians 5:15–17 GWT)

God both exhorts and cautions us to live by the truth. Do you need to change some of the pictures you carry about faith?

THE AUTOGRAPHED PICTURE

The bigger picture provided us with a panoramic view of faith as it is defined and practiced. But something else that needs to be understood is the *personal* way that faith blesses and enriches our lives. I call this the autographed picture because God has put our names on what our faith looks like. It's that individual. It's that intimate.[7] For each of us who endeavors to make faith in God what our lives look like, we can anticipate its effect on our lives in the following ways.

FAITH IS A BLESSING

Faith has blessed God's people throughout the history of humankind. This world may chide, rebuke, or even persecute people of faith, but God never abandons those who choose to have faith in Him. The promise He made to Israel, recorded in Deuteronomy 31:8, when they were finally ready to enter the Promised Land, still holds true for people of faith today: "The Lord himself goes before you and will be with you; He will never leave you nor forsake you. Do not be afraid; do not be discouraged."

FAITH PROTECTS US AND GIVES US SECURITY

In addition to all, taking up the shield of faith with which you will be able to extinguish all the flaming arrows of the evil one. (Ephesians 6:16)

The epistle of 1 John teaches that "greater is He that is in you than he that is in the world." Faith makes this a practical reality.

Faith gives us victory over the experiences of our past, current circumstances, and challenges to come.

For whatever is born of God overcomes the world,
and this is the victory that has overcome the world,
our faith. Who is the one who overcomes the world,
but he who believes that Jesus is the Son of God.
(1 John 5:4–5)

When we trust in God to be at work in us to "will and act in
order to fulfill his good purpose," as Philippians instructs, we receive
confidence and contentment that only God can provide.

Faith brings happiness, joy, praise, and wholeness to our lives.

Although you have never seen Christ, you love him. You don't
see him now, but you believe in him. You are extremely happy with
joy and praise that can hardly be expressed in words as you obtain
the salvation that is the goal of your faith. (1 Peter 1:8–9)

With some of His last words to His disciples before His death,
Jesus told His disciples in John's gospel that "I have told you these
things, so that in me you may have peace. In this world you will have
trouble. But take heart! I have overcome the world."[6] God brings
an inner abundance of blessings to our lives according to our faith.

FAITH DEFINES WHO WE ARE

"If you live by what I say, you are truly my disciples" (John
8:31 GWT).

What we place our faith in determines our character, values,
priorities, and purposes. It determines what we worship and who we
follow. Living the words of Jesus is godly faith.[8]

These faith photographs reveal a tapestry-like picture of how we
are to live and for what we are to live. While the fibers that compose
this tapestry apply to all of Jesus's followers, each of us, with the
help and power of God, has the awesome responsibility to weave
it in the individual way that God had created us and called us for

serving in His kingdom. Like the believers mentioned in chapter 11 of Hebrews, the photograph of our life's tapestry of faith is included in God's family album.

———————

This picture of godly faith is rich and comprehensive in its subject matter. It takes understanding, effort, and time to bring its meaning and relevance to us into clear focus. For this to happen, we need to make a covenant with the essential and principal consideration of this chapter: Your life can be a picture of genuine, godly faith. Take your faith in God seriously. Value and guard it. Try to understand and grow in it. Make it your life's priority.

CHAPTER 4

THE STRUCTURE OF FAITH

The secret of change is to focus all of your energy not on fighting the old but on building the new.

—*Socrates*

I have been a professional furniture maker and restorer for almost five decades. Over that time, I have made hundreds of chairs and restored thousands. Chairs come in all kinds of shapes, styles, colors, materials, and levels of embellishment. They are such an ordinary, everyday item that we may never think about how a chair does its job or why it is made the way it is. Despite their variety, monetary value, and age, we trust the reliability of their function because they earn that every time we sit down on them.

Early in my career, I developed a curiosity over how an average dining room chair can support a person ten to twenty times its weight over decades of use. I have studied much of what has been written about chair design's geometry and engineering principles. I have found that over hundreds of years, designers, mathematicians, and engineers have concluded that a chair with four legs with a stretcher that connects them all together is the most stable, strong, and enduring. Some antique chairs seemed light and delicate, yet they were strong and dependable even though they were more than 250 years old!

I have come to respect chairs as an engineering marvel. One of the pioneers of modern architecture, Ludwig mies van der Rohe, concurred: "A chair is a very difficult object. A skyscraper is almost easier. That is why Chippendale is famous."[1]

The simplicity of their design belies their engineering sophistication and strength.

This assembly of four legs with a stretcher makes up the chair's base that supports the seat. When correctly assembled, it forms a structure of remarkable stability and longevity. Independent of each other, they do not provide strength and stability. Their relationship with each other and how they are connected accomplishes this. Everything above the seat—the back, sides, and arms, are important for the personal appeal, value, and comfort they provide, but they do little to increase the strength and stability of the chair. Without the base supporting them, they are useless.

A chair's design begins with an idea, a conceptualization of what the chair will look like. Much thought and effort go into determining the style, proportions, materials, aesthetics, and decorative embellishments. But every aspect of these design considerations is constrained by one thing. And that is the necessary requirement that the chair can perform its rudimentary function—that of being able to be sat in!

A chair needs four trustworthy legs to support the seat to perform its function and fulfill its primary reason for existing. The stretcher provides the means of connecting them to combine and enhance their individual strength, evenly distributes the stress applied to them, and keeps them in place. Without this foundation, as beautiful, unique, and impressive as a chair may be, it has no functional purpose or useful meaning. Other than an appealing appearance, it benefits no one.

Consider the parallels here to our lives. We begin with a "design" or conceptualization of what we want our lives to look like. We consider our education and career path and our income goals relative to this. We picture the type of person we want to marry, how many children we will have, and where we will live. We determine what is essential about our physical appearance and what we need to do to stay healthy. We try to ascertain our character and moral values and what philanthropic efforts we deem worthwhile. We try to find a meaningful rationale for who we are and what we do. The list could go on. Yet, like a poorly designed and constructed chair, a life without a trustworthy foundation becomes something that might be attractive to look at but lacks genuine strength, structural integrity, usefulness, and, especially, purpose.

THE METAPHOR OF THE CHAIR

Design and construction metaphors are used throughout the Bible[2] to help us visualize the process of building faith. Consider the man who built his house upon the rock versus the man who built his house upon the sand. Jesus used this metaphor to illustrate the significance and consequences of the truth He taught in the Sermon on the Mount. Apostle Paul used the image of the wise master builder to address building the foundation of the church with truth, integrity, and wisdom. And Isaiah used the metaphor of God as the potter and us as the clay to point out our need and dependence on Him to shape our lives. Even in secular writings, the Athenian philosopher Plato used furniture as a metaphor to illustrate the existence of virtuous ideals in his dialogue "The Form of the Good."[3]

The design and construction of a chair provide a three-part visual representation of how we design and construct our lives. First, the chair's base represents the foundation that supports our life. The integrity of this foundation determines the strength, purpose, and character of who we are. Second, the seat symbolizes our soul or who we are—our mind, heart, personality, preferences, character, opinions, and aspirations. The seat of the chair is functional and fulfills its purpose in direct correlation to the integrity of the base. Third, that which is above the seat—the back, arms, and other parts—represents what we do with our lives—our education, family, careers, recreation, and pursuits. And like the seat, what we do with our lives is functional and fulfilling relative to the foundation supporting it.

FAITH HAS FOUR LEGS AND A STRETCHER

God has given us five components to build our lives upon, like a chair's base. Each of these is necessary to bring us into a relationship of believing faith with God. And, like the base of a chair, they were never designed to be independent of each other. Without their being correctly connected to each other and working together, our faith is compromised and, at worst, is nonfunctional. Because the source of these five components is Almighty God, the creator and author of life, we can trust and depend on their integrity. Their intrinsic strength is securely established in God's meaningful way and has designed and engineered human life. When they are correctly assembled and firmly attached to each other, they provide us with an enduring and genuinely spiritual foundation for our character, values, moral compass, and purpose in this life. They are the necessary and primary elements of what is called godly faith.

And like the base of a chair, the simplicity of God's design for faith belies its sophistication and strength.

THE FIVE COMPONENTS OF FAITH

Using our chair metaphor, faith is represented by the properly connected whole of five components characterized by four legs and a stretcher. The legs represent:

truth

love

fellowship

The faith disciplines

The stretcher represents the connecting element of being spiritually minded.

Genuine faith consists of no less.

The drawing below illustrates the legs and stretcher that compose our faith—the base upon which we build our lives.

The Leg of Truth

The Leg of Fellowship

The Leg of Love

The Stretcher of Being Spiritually Minded

The Leg of the Faith Disciplines

Each of these components is of equal value and relevance to faith. We can sometimes make the mistake of prioritizing one or two of them above or to the neglect of the others. For instance, one may argue that 1 Corinthians 13 makes the point that without the love of God, everything else is just an annoying noise (my paraphrase). While this is undoubtedly true, to live by love alone has never been God's intention, given the emphasis that scriptures place on these other elements of faith. Each of these, or aspects of them, is mentioned hundreds of times in the Bible.

We should value and pursue them equally because: Truth alone can be harsh and uncompromising. Yet, without it, our understanding of whom God is, His will for us, and our relationship with Him are entirely elusive. We have no basis for evaluating the genuine godliness of our direction in life. Truth illuminates our concept of purpose, motives, and, most importantly, living the way we ought to please God and develop true faith. Truth not only tells us what faith is but also what faith does.

Love alone can be misguided and directionless and be drawn into emotional compromises and insecurity. But without it, we are bereft of the ability to change our hearts and repent of sin. Most importantly, our relationship with God is severely compromised because love is at the core of that relationship. Without the love of God, we cannot manifest the humility, forgiveness, empathy, and will to give of ourselves that engenders cherished and fulfilling relationships.

Fellowship alone provides no personal accountability for our character, behavior, and responsibility to live according to the truth and with love and use God's gifts. But without it, we are left powerless to overcome so many circumstances in life that require God's divine intervention. The Holy Spirit is our personal connection to His omnipotence, omniscience, and omnipresence. And fellowship with one another provides us with circumstances to put truth and love into practice.

The faith disciplines alone become a self-serving and meaningless religious exercise. They make the truth, love, and the Holy Spirit a living reality to us. However, without our faithful practice of them, we will never grow spiritually.

And if we neglect the godly way of thinking about these aspects of our faith—that stretcher that connects them—we fail to unite them in the way that makes our faith complete, strong, and stable.

These five components make up what godly faith is composed of and requires. Understanding their true purpose and how they function together enables us to assemble a foundation of holy faith upon which to build our lives. If we do so on this foundation, God has given us the freedom and capability to live in an appealing, enjoyable, and fulfilling way.

THE PERSONIFICATION OF FAITH

When I was an apprentice furniture maker, I had to learn the process of developing the numerous skills required to make a chair. It took education, time, repetition, patience, discipline, and humility. Proficiency in some skills came relatively easily, while it was challenging in others. Some I mastered; some I'm still working on. Fortunately, I had a teacher who could instruct me with patience and understanding.

We have the ultimate master teacher and the perfect example of what faith looks like in the person of Jesus Christ. As His apprentices, we take confidence in knowing that He never gives up on us or is unwilling to help us. He has a vision for what we can achieve and become as we grow in faith, even when we don't. He gave His life for our faith. To look at the life of Jesus is to look at faith.

He epitomized the five aspects of faith:

He gave us the truth that sets us free to understand and live by faith.

He exemplified the love of God in every way and toward everyone.

He sent the comforter—the Holy Spirit—to guide, empower, and bring us into a relationship of fellowship with God and His family.

He showed us how to mature and become strong in faith through the disciplines.

He demonstrated that by being intentionally spiritually minded, we connect all these together to complete the foundation of our faith.

Jesus personified a holy life consecrated to God, a life of believing faith. His life is the example we imitate to do the same.

The legs of truth, love, fellowship, and the faith disciplines are not shaped by God alone. Our faith is precisely that, *our* faith. God wants us to take ownership of it. Jesus has exemplified how to live it. He has given us the blueprint of its structure in His Word. He has empowered us with His love. He has given us His Spirit to guide us. We have the fellowship of the body of Christ to help us mature in it and hold one another accountable for its authenticity. What is important now is that we try to use what God has provided for us to build our faith to support our lives in the way He intended.

In the chapters that follow, we will look at these components of faith, what they mean individually, their relationship with each other, and how they are connected to form the foundation of a godly life—a life of Christlike faith. The order of the chapters is in no way related to their importance or priority. Each is vital to faith.

When I had that conversation with the rancher at the rest stop along the interstate, unknown to me at the time was that I was being introduced to the structure of faith: the winsomeness of the truth, the love of God shown to me from this stranger by speaking into my life, the supernatural power of the Holy Spirit at work to draw my heart to fellowship with God, the idea that there are specific efforts that I could make that would help me grow spiritually, and how the way I think unites them in an intentional and practicable way.

That incident speaks to what is the vital consideration for this chapter:

An accurate and understandable structure for our faith journey provides us with precise directions and measurable progress. It is composed of truth, love, fellowship, the faith disciplines, and being spiritually minded.

CHAPTER 5

ASSESSING FAITH

Examine yourselves to see if your faith is genuine. Test yourselves.

—2 Corinthians 13:5 (NLT)

Several years ago, I examined a piece of furniture for a client to determine its overall condition and restoration needs. It was a superbly composed desk with pleasing proportions, masterful construction, complex carvings, and moldings, and was made with highly figured mahogany woods.

Typically, when I assess the condition of any furniture item, my primary concern is that it can perform its intended function. I look to see that the individual components have structural integrity, that the joints that hold these components together are secure and stable, if any of the decorative elements are missing, and whether the overall appearance reflects the maker's original intent. If any of these conditions are compromised, I determine the cause and develop a plan for correcting them.

But aside from the desk's aesthetic importance and physical condition, this client wanted me to investigate other aspects of the desk. It had been in his family for generations and therefore had particular importance to him. Aside from its restoration needs, he was interested to find out about its history and chain of ownership.

When I begin an assessment like this, I start by asking the object to talk to me. I start the conversation by asking it to tell me a little about itself. As I unhurriedly study it from a short distance away, it begins to talk. Because of my training and expertise, I understand its language.

Its overall style, proportions, decorative elements, and primary woods tell me it was made in the late 1700s and probably from eastern Virginia or North Carolina. As I look closer at its vernacular construction methods and the secondary woods used, it confirms an eastern North Carolina origin. The wear, ink stains, and pen impressions on its writing surface and severely worn drawer runners tell me it was in constant use for a long time and served an important function to its owner. It was not purely a decorative object. From these and other details, it begins to tell me its story, and I was able to narrow down its probable place of manufacture.

I began to look for signatures, labels, or other identification markings. Finding these on pieces of antique furniture is very rare. But hidden from cursory view, I found what I was looking for on the inside edge of one of the drawer dividers. Written with a pencil in eighteenth-century-style handwriting was not only the name of the maker but the date, location, and customer name for which it was made—the same as my client's! When I explained to him what I had found—the signature of the maker and that the desk was originally built for his family—he was elated, and the value of the desk increased dramatically to him. Not in dollars but in the story it told about his family from over two hundred years ago.

This detailed inspection culminated in identifying some important information about the desk that had been unknown for generations. Over the centuries, dozens of people have looked at it, but some of its most unique values and meaning remained hidden because they didn't do it closely enough and intentionally.

It makes the point that for something to be personally meaningful, we must closely look at it to determine its value.

IF YOUR FAITH COULD SPEAK

Just like this desk, our faith tells a story. But this one is about the ongoing journey of our spiritual growth and maturity. The condition of our faith has something to say to us, but we need to look and listen. The purpose of assessing our faith is to determine how genuine it is, and from there, we can seek direction for growth.

I'll ask you some questions I often ask myself:

What story would a close inspection of your faith tell about you?

What would it say about your understanding and value of the truth?

What would it bring to light about your love for God and for people?

Would it describe a solid and personal relationship of fellowship with God and people?

What would it disclose about the importance to you of practicing the faith disciplines?

To what degree would it describe the Christlike way you think?

Would your signature be on it, documenting that you have taken ownership of it?

These questions require contemplation. In appendix 2, I have provided some suggestions for when and how to do this that I hope will be as helpful to you as they have been to me.

ASSESSING FAITH REQUIRES GOD'S INVOLVEMENT

Unlike a physical object, our faith is not composed of natural or man-made materials that can be quickly repaired or strengthened. And we cannot rely solely on our own ability or skill. We are dealing with the condition of the human heart—a heart created by God, by His design, and in His image. Consequently, God defines the integrity of the materials that compose our faith. Considering this, our humility and surrender to the will of God, plus the transforming power of the Holy Spirit, governs, energizes, and validates our efforts in the forward movement and longevity of our faith.

There can be no true faith absent the active presence of God. The condition of our faith is not exclusively up to us. And the same holds true as we assess our faith.

Author Kristen Wetherell,[1] writing on The Gospel Coalition's website for Christian Living,[2] makes the point that:

God's searching ministry is accomplished by His Spirit. We don't examine ourselves by our own wisdom and knowledge but by His revealing work. We can pray: Almighty God, you know every corner of my being, far more than I could ever know. By your Spirit, give me eyes to see what's going on in my heart and mind. Such knowledge is too wonderful for me but not for you. Search me and know me, God.

Self-examination isn't ultimately empowered by us, but by the One who made us—and we can trust Him to use what He reveals for our good.

The enemy's goal is to get us stuck looking at ourselves—our flaws, our failures, our fears—when we need to look *away* from ourselves to Jesus. Therefore, we need the Savior! Yes, we should mourn our sin and feel the depths of our rebellion against a holy God—that is good and right. But Satan wants that to be the *end*. Thankfully, it's not the end for those united by faith to the Advocate, the righteous one.

Without the recognition and dependence of God's active involvement in our lives, no matter how strong our will and intentionality of our efforts, our time spent assessing our faith will turn into an end in itself and leave us navel-gazing discouraged.

START WITH YOUR HEART

Any evaluation of our faith starts with an assessment of our hearts. When we dive into assessing our faith, we're going into deep waters. You want to get beneath the superficial concerns of life and get to what matters in your heart—that deepest part of your soul that makes you ... you! The holy scriptures have much to say about the condition and importance of our hearts.[3]

> Trust in the Lord with all your heart, and do not lean on your own understanding. In all your ways acknowledge him, and he will make straight your paths. (Proverbs 3:5–6 ESV)

This verse speaks to issues deep within us—issues of trust, issues of priorities, and issues of what defines our lives. How important is it, then, to follow through on the admonition given in Proverbs[4] to keep or "guard" our hearts. Because, as our physical hearts pump the oxygen and nutrients that our bodies need to survive and function, our spiritual hearts need to be kept healthy to pump spiritual nutrients into our faith.

Guarding our hearts begins with choosing the way we allow ourselves to think. No one can control the way you think. No one can protect your heart for you. What we allow our minds to feed on will determine what thoughts will germinate, grow, and eventually produce the fruit of their nature.

It's a principle of growth that Jesus made in the gospel of Matthew:

> Likewise, every good tree bears good fruit, but a bad tree bears bad fruit. A good tree cannot bear bad fruit, and a bad tree cannot bear good fruit. Every tree that does not bear good fruit is cut down and

thrown into the fire. Thus, by their fruit you will recognize them. (Matthew 7:16–20)

The way we think is governed to a large degree by what we expose our minds to. That's why it's important to watch over what we read, look at, watch on various media, and the types of conversations and relationships in which we engage. Our thought life is the entranceway to our hearts, and we need to guard what we allow to enter.

ASSESS YOUR LOCATION ON YOUR FAITH JOURNEY

We are all at various locations on our journey of faith. An essential aspect of evaluating our spiritual life is understanding where we are now and where we are attempting to go. This enables us to put our faith in perspective, as discussed in chapter 11.

Below is a list of what I call thresholds of spiritual growth. They're not clear-cut from one step to the next because often we are strong in parts of one threshold and weaker in others. At times we take two steps forward and one step back. What is important is that we see a measurable movement toward becoming spiritually grounded in our faith. By "spiritually grounded," I mean that we reflect a loving and obedient relationship with God and surrender and trust our lives to His will over ours. As we evaluate where we are in this spiritual movement, we can seek out help where we need it and be thankful for (not proud of) our progress.

I provide this list with the solemn understanding that I am not the author of the defining attributes of spiritual growth! It is incomplete and serves only as an example. These thresholds are *my* understanding of how spiritual development might be measured from what is written in the New Testament of the Bible. They are one of the ways I have tried to define and measure it in my life and recognize it in others.[5] I'm not big on following lists. I must be careful that they don't turn into a mechanical routine for me. Nonetheless, we must start somewhere, and you may need to add other helpful measures.

If you were to describe the current state of your spirituality, would you say these things?

EXPLORING

You're contemplating the spiritual purpose of life and the possibility of an intelligent creator behind it.

You're investigating what truth means and its relevance to God.

You're concerned about what happens after this life as we know it.

You're beginning to learn about Jesus Christ—what His life means to you; considering what He taught, if what the Bible says about Him is true; and if you can trust His words to be dependable.

ACCEPTING

You accept Jesus Christ as the way, the truth, and the life, even though you know you have a way to understand what this means in living it out.

You have decided He is worth following, that what He taught and lived is the truth and is the way you want to live.

GROWING

You increasingly trust God's promises in His word.

You are changing values to align with those of God.

Your prayer life is becoming meaningful and a time that is precious to you.

The faith disciplines are becoming part of your daily life.
You're reaching out to others for help.
You see spiritual fruit being produced in your life.

MATURING

You are intentional in your thoughts about and conversations with God.

You are secure in knowing that God loves you unconditionally.
You forgive and love others unconditionally.
You seek out opportunities to do good for humanity.
You are freeing yourself from judging those who are different than you.

You are at peace and confident about your faith with others.
You have no idols in your life.

SPIRITUALLY GROUNDED

Your life is centered daily on living a godly life.

This list is far from complete. There is no pecking order of value or importance here. All these steps are significant, and one builds upon another. God loves and values all people because we are all His creation and not because of our spiritual understanding and maturity. They don't earn us any points with God or make Him love us more. Becoming spiritually grounded in the way we live is for our fulfillment and blessing—and it does impact this world positively and helpfully. Just like we as parents have joy in the growth and fulfillment of our children, God has joy with each step we take in spiritual maturity.

———————

This chapter contains a lot of questions! It can be challenging to take the time to ask, contemplate, and respond to them meaningfully. I again refer you to appendix 2 as a format for incorporating a helpful process to ponder and answer them. Applying these methods to your spiritual formation will develop a clearer picture of your location on your journey of faith now and an intentional vision of the following steps to take.

What is important to be mindful of from this chapter is: Even more important than the time and effort we spend assessing our health, finances, personal goals, and so many other areas of our lives, understanding and stewarding our faith needs constant attention. With God's help, the support of our spiritual family, and pure-hearted engagement on our part, our faith can be nurtured into maturity.

— PART 2 —

CONSTRUCTING
YOUR FAITH

INTRODUCTION

God is not responsible for your faith—you are. He will not make you know the truth, love Him or people, control your fellowship with Him or others, make you practice the disciplines, or take over your thoughts. The responsibility, effort, intentionality, and consistency we involve ourselves with these activities is up to us. God is there to help us through the power of His Spirit, the mediation of His Son, and the truth of His Word. But He requires our genuine involvement.

Scriptures reveal five components that faith is comprised of that we are to be diligent in developing as we progress on our journey of faith. As we understand what they are composed of and assemble them into an integral part of the way we live, we build a foundation for our lives that is fruitful, powerful, dependable, and, most importantly, pleasing to God.

CHAPTER 6

THE LEG OF TRUTH

To risk reputation and affection for the truth's sake is so demanding that to do it constantly you will need a degree of moral principle that only the Spirit of God can work in you.

—*Alistair Begg*

God has provided us with a path to Him. He is not absent from us as we begin the journey toward Him. Even though He may seem far off at times, He is always before us, and as we follow His directions, we get closer and closer to Him. Yet, how do we know this, and how does it become real to us?

Like every journey, this one has a beginning: the path to God begins with truth.

"What is truth?"[1] is the infamous question asked of Jesus by the Roman prefect, Pontius Pilate. The question was not a new one. It has been discussed, debated, and written about throughout the millennia and continues today. Finding the answer to this question is one of the most life-shaping quests we undertake and is vital to true faith. It deserves serious inquiry and contemplation. And the most important and defining question to be answered to arrive at the truth is, "What is its source?"

VALIDATING THE TRUTH

During a recent television interview, an author made the point that all religions, philosophies, and world views are equally valid and justified. She asserted that no absolute truth applied to everyone equally. She contended that spiritual truth was relative and that her truth, my truth, and anyone else's truth are equally legitimate. However, there was one qualifier, one absolute, that she insisted was required of all these viewpoints. And that was, "as long as it doesn't hurt anyone else."

As I sat there with my eyes rolling, I kept hollering at the interviewer on TV, saying, "Ask her the question! Ask her the question!" What was this question? If there is no such thing as absolute truth, and all truth is relative to each individual's personal values, why did she require this one absolute to validate all beliefs? She, as well as the interviewer, was apparently oblivious to her contradiction of terms.

So goes the conversation about spiritual truth in twenty-first century Western culture! Absolute truth has been replaced with relative truth. Truth has become highly selective and, at worst, all but abandoned and disconnected from reality. Opinions about it are rife with contradictions and often devolve into thoughtless nonsense.

The author's remarks illustrate a striking contrast in beliefs as to the origin of truth and why the source of it is so important. Relative truth recognizes the individual as its source and portends to have no absolutes outside of the individual. It maintains that every person has the means within them to construct their own spiritual reality. It is a type of pantheism that acknowledges everyone as their own god. All that matters is what the individual likes or values. The conclusions of this viewpoint of truth change as the values and perspectives of the person making them change. What is true one day may become false the next. Often, the motives for this change are based upon selfish personal desires and avoiding accountability for their behavior.

The fact that something appears to be true because of a feeling, human appetites, popular opinions, the charisma of an authority figure, or even a respected scholar's writings and intellectual notions does not guarantee its validity. We must grow beyond living according to what the truth appears to be and arrive at a place of genuine understanding.

Vague notions of scriptural truths, coupled with fuzzy understandings of how those truths apply in real situations, lead to a Christianity with neither eyes nor a heart: it cannot see where it is going and doesn't really care that much either. As Aristotle said, "Generalities are the refuge of the weak mind."[2]

We disregard this point at our own peril. Scriptures speak to this frequently.[3]

> For the time will come when people will not put up with sound doctrine. Instead, to suit their own desires, they will gather around them a great number of teachers to say what their itching ears want to hear. They will turn their ears away from the truth and turn aside to myths. (2 Timothy 4:3–4)

Truth as God explains it in the Bible is very different. It is based upon Him and only Him and recognizes that only He is the source of what is real and true. God doesn't change because He learned something new, is in a bad mood, or overestimates what He is capable of. He is not worried about what people think of Him. He does not have questions about reality because He created reality. All

His words to us can be trusted, and what He says is true today and will be true tomorrow.[4]

> The entirety of your word is truth, and all your righteous judgments endure forever. (Psalm 119:160)

When pursuing the truth, God clarifies that He is the source of it. He points out that our conviction about the veracity of the truth He speaks is based upon our reverence of Him and recognition of Him as the source. It is not inherently within us. And like any body of knowledge, truth needs to be learned from a source outside of us. The popular notion that truth is found within ourselves is no more reasonable than looking inside ourselves to find the knowledge of history, medicine, law, or geography. The reputation and credibility of our schools are essential in selecting where we pursue our secular education. How much more significant is the source from which we seek spiritual truth!

> Teach me your way, O LORD, that I may walk in your truth. Give me an undivided heart, that I may fear your name. (Psalm 86:11)

Notice the emphasis on God in this verse:
Your way, Lord
Your truth, Lord
Your name, Lord
On our journey of faith, it is the truth that God provides us in scripture that gives us the directions that guide us to Him. And because God is the source of what forms the leg of truth in constructing our faith, we can depend upon its strength and reliability.

FAITH REQUIRES TRUTH

In sixteenth century England, a popular idiom today developed out
of a reference to chairs and stools. Each time a leg was removed, it
would provide less support to the person sitting on it, and eventually,
the phrase "you don't have a leg to stand on" was born.[5] Without
truth, faith doesn't have a leg to stand on. Without the truth provided
by God in His Word, we are left with anecdotal opinions that don't
support what faith is and means.

> Consequently, faith comes from hearing the
> message, and the message is heard through the word
> about Christ. (Romans 10:17)

Unlike the author's opinion mentioned before, the "message"
referred to here is not found within us or from any secular source,
no matter how appealing or erudite it may appear. It is in the words
of scripture. Truth clarifies what or whom we are to have faith in.
Without the truth of God, there can be no faith in God.

Knowing what scripture says about God enables us to have the
true image of Him that faith requires. God's word explains His
character, His desires, and the magnitude of His love for us. It makes
known His power and knowledge and defines and clarifies His will.
It describes His purposes in the mighty acts of the creation of the
earth and the heavens, the beauty, complexity of nature, and all life
forms. His word gives us an accurate understanding of God's nature,
personality, thoughts and feelings, eternal plans, and worldview
through the truth of His inspired word.

No matter how beautiful and appealing the leg of a chair is
shaped, it must be made of material with inherent integrity to
dependably perform its function. Our leg of truth has integrity to
the degree that it consists of what God reveals to us in His word. Its

strength is compromised by anything less. Genuine faith requires genuine truth.

TREASURING THE TRUTH

What do you treasure? What makes your treasure valuable? Have you ever considered the scriptures as a treasure? God has given us the most powerful and holy words ever written. How significant the reverence and value we place on the word of God must be!

> God's word is living and active. It is sharper than any two-edged sword and cuts as deep as the place where soul and spirit meet, the place where joints and marrow meet. God's word judges a person's thoughts and intentions. (Hebrews 4:12 GWT)

Considering this, we should examine ourselves and ask if any of these situations apply to us:

Do we consider the Bible as God speaking to us in a living and active way?

Do we pick and choose what we think is important or what applies to us?

Do we need to repent over some of our attitudes toward the scriptures?

> God's divine power has given us everything we need for life and for godliness. This power was given to us through knowledge of the one who called us by his own glory and integrity. Through his glory and integrity, he has given us his promises that are of the highest value. Through these promises you will share in the divine nature because you have escaped

the corruption that sinful desires cause in the world.
(2 Peter 1:3–4)

God has primarily revealed Himself to us through words. When you think about it, we all live and die by words. We have the responsibility to choose which words those are going to be. Will they be God's words or the words of man? The godliness we seek is revealed to us initially through the knowledge that God has provided to us.

> In contrast to the insipid worth relativism places on words, listen to what God has to say about His words: "In the beginning was the word, and the word was with God, and the Word was God (John 1:1)."

If God's word is God, what value do we place upon it? We don't set the Bible on an altar and worship it, but at the least, we should revere it as holy words from a holy God.

> And the words of the Lord are flawless, like silver purified in a crucible, like gold refined seven times. (Psalm 12:6)

The truth we have is one of the most valuable gifts God has given us. We must take responsibility for filling our minds with it.

In the gospel of John, Jesus reveals one of the most valuable attributes of divine truth: freedom!

> Then you will know the truth, and the truth will set you free. (John 8:32)

Everyone treasures freedom, yet not everyone finds it. Sometimes, when the truth finally pierces our hearts and opens our eyes, we become aware of prisons we didn't even know we were in. The Jewish Pharisees that Jesus was speaking to mistakenly considered themselves free because they were not physically enslaved. But Jesus was referring to slavery that was much more consequential and pervasive—the slavery of sin. Unlike the relative truth in popular culture that prioritizes the freedom *to* sin, Jesus's truth frees us *from* sin. And in the final analysis, sin is not true freedom. It is an emotional prison of conscience.

The Message Bible beautifully explains this freedom in Romans.

> As long as you did what you felt like doing, ignoring God, you didn't have to bother with right thinking or right living, or right *anything* for that matter. But do you call that a free life? What did you get out of it? Nothing you're proud of now. Where did it get you? A dead end. But now that you've found you don't have to listen to sin tell you what to do and have discovered the delight of listening to God telling you, what a surprise! A whole, healed, put-together life right now, with more and more of life on the way! Work hard for sin your whole life and your pension is death. But God's gift is *real life*, eternal life, delivered by Jesus, our Master. (Romans 6:20–23)

If you value true freedom, the freedom only Christ can bring, God's word will be a treasure.

THE PERSONIFICATION OF TRUTH

When we consider the completed works of Jesus, we primarily recognize and honor His miraculous work of salvation, redemption, love, forgiveness, and eternal life. Yet, the Gospel of John also brings to light one of the greatest gifts that Jesus gave us—the living truth! He was able to provide us with the truth because He was the truth, the living word of God.

> The word became flesh and made his dwelling among us. We have seen his glory, the glory of the one and only Son, who came from the Father, full of grace and truth. (John 1:14)

> We also know that the Son of God has come and has given us the understanding to know him who is true. And we are in him who is true by being in his Son Jesus Christ. He is the true God and eternal life. (1 John 5:20)

As followers of Jesus, we have access to an example, a personification of what truth looks like that far exceeds what came before Him. To look at the life of Jesus is to look at the truth.[6]

> Jesus answered I am the way and the truth and the life. No one comes to the Father except through me. If you really know me, you will know my Father as well. From now on, you do know him and have seen him. (John 14:6)

This truth that Jesus exemplified reveals God to us. He is the ultimate living model of truth. Because He personifies the truth, what is shown here speaks to far more than mere knowledge of the truth but a relationship with the truth.

OUR RELATIONSHIP WITH THE TRUTH

Imagine that we were briefly introduced at a party. I watched what you were doing and overheard you speaking. What you said piqued my interest in getting to know you. So, I went to your spouse and some of your friends and asked them to tell me all about you. They had diverse opinions, and their descriptions of you varied in complexity and experience. While these conversations might give an apt description of their opinion of you, even if lengthy and detailed, would you and I have what would be considered an intimate or even personal relationship? Of course not! I might know a lot about you at best, but I wouldn't really know you personally. Yet, it seems that this is how so many go about developing their relationship with God, arguably the most important relationship we will ever have.

Additionally, we don't nurture a strong friendship with someone by sitting in their house once a week and listening to another person talk about them. Likewise, merely sitting in church and listening to the Sunday sermon is not what brings us into an endearing relationship with God. I don't mean to demean or dismiss the many godly aspects of church attendance. It is an essential component of our Christian life. But its central purpose is in worship. How can we genuinely worship something we don't have a close and intentional relationship with? Wouldn't that be foolish or even dangerous?

Also, we don't get to know people by praying about it. Faith is, in its essence, about a relationship. Like any endearing, strong, and meaningful human connection, our relationship with God develops through conversation and time spent together—getting to know each other personally. It takes a concerted, committed, and transparent effort on our part, fueled by a desire for and value of that relationship. And truth defines the capabilities, requirements, and responsibilities of the two parties involved in this relationship: us and God.

The scriptures are, in effect, God speaking personally to us about who He is and who we are to Him. Consider the words of David, a man after God's own heart:

> You have searched me, Lord, and you know me. You know when I sit and when I rise; you perceive my thoughts from afar. You discern my going out and my lying down; you are familiar with all my ways. Before a word is on my tongue you, Lord, know it completely. (Psalm 139:1–4)

God knows us intimately. Our challenge is taking the time and trying to know Him. Not just listening to the words of others that tell us about Him or describe their relationship with Him, as inspiring as they may be. We get to know Him by meeting with Him in His word. God is found in His words.[7] They are the basis of building our understanding of and relationship with Him.

If we desire to be close to God and develop an enduring faith in Him, the truth of His word will show us how. Consider the heartfelt testimony of someone who loved and treasured His word.

> I seek you with all my heart. Do not let me stray from your commands. I have hidden your word in my heart that I might not sin against you. Praise be to you, Lord, teach me your decrees. With my lips I recount all the laws that come from your mouth. I rejoice in following your statutes as one rejoices in great riches. I meditate on your precepts and consider your ways. I delight in your decrees, I will not neglect your word. (Psalm 119:10–16)

Does this describe your relationship with the truth?

The ultimate purpose of God's truth is to bring all of humankind into a living and genuine relationship with Him. Scriptures give us the truth that a genuine faith relationship with Him requires. How precious they are! Jesus, the living word, exemplified the ultimate example of faith that we might imitate. He shows us how that is lived out on a day-to-day basis, personally and with every human, including you and me!

What makes truth relevant to the structure of our faith is also the main point of this chapter: truth gives us the blueprint for building faith.

CHAPTER 7

THE LEG OF LOVE

God bestows His blessings without discrimination. The followers of Jesus are children of God, and they should manifest the family likeness by doing good to all, even to those who deserve the opposite. [1]

—*F. F. Bruce*

As a ten-year-old boy overwhelmed with curiosity, I stood next to my father's brand new 1963 dark blue Oldsmobile 98. The car was a wonder of modern technology and gadgetry. Of particular interest to me were the remote-controlled outside mirrors. They were not the electric kind that we have today, but the kind that was adjustable by a toggle switch on the driver's side door that moved the position of the mirrors with a wire cable.

The desire to figure out how this worked consumed me! So, I began to unscrew the driver's side mirror, turning it counterclockwise on its support arm. To my great surprise and alarm, the mirror's housing was spring-loaded, and once it was loose, it popped off the support arm and dangled by the cable on the side of the door. Try as I might, I was unable to reattach the mirror.

The consequences of my actions began to dawn on me, and

they were not pretty. My father loved this car. He had talked about buying it for months, and he had owned it for three days. He had made it very clear that my siblings and I were not to touch the car when he was not present.

I began to get sick to my stomach as I considered my father's reaction to what I had done. I decided to retreat to my bedroom and get back in bed. As I passed my mother in the kitchen, I told her I didn't feel well and was going to lie down. So, I went to my room, got into my bed, curled up into a fetal position, and pulled the covers over my head.

After what seemed like hours, there was a knock at the door, and my father came in. He said that mom had told him I was not feeling well, and he wanted to see if I was all right. He came and sat down on the bed next to me and put his hand on my forehead as if checking to see if I had a fever. After a few moments of silence, he said he knew about what I did to the car mirror. He told me he had fixed it, and it was working just fine. He said he understood my curiosity about how things work, but that I should first ask him for his help so he could show me in the future. He told me not to worry about it and that he forgave me and loved me. He got up from the bed, said that he hoped I would be feeling better soon, and left my room.

It was then that I experienced miraculous and immediate healing of my illness! What my father told me lifted an enormous weight off me. I got out of bed, went back outside, and began to enjoy my Saturday morning without a care in the world.

As I have pondered the life lesson of this incident over the ensuing years, it has made one thing very clear to me: fear and guilt are prisons. They are antithetical to peace, joy, and freedom. They can have a devastating effect on us, even to the point of making us physically ill. In extreme cases, people have taken their lives because of an inability to deal with them. But here's the good news.

As powerful as fear and guilt are, their strength is toothless in the face of love.

When it comes to faith, it is the leg of love that emancipates us from the prisons of our past, the guilt of our mistakes, bad choices, and failures. It enables us to live with peacefulness and confidence in ourselves and our relationship with God. It gives purpose, provides value, and brings unity to our relationships with others.

VALIDATING LOVE

Love is a subject that has probably had more books, songs, poems, and discussions about it than any other topic known to humanity. It has been studied and analyzed over thousands of years and yet is often gravely misunderstood and dysfunctional in how it is practiced. Its purpose can seem capricious and fickle considering that in the name of love, both beautiful acts of selflessness and horrific acts of selfishness have happened. Considering how people are mistreated, discriminated against, lonely, and emotionally, physically, and even spiritually abused, it's very evident that we suffer from a love problem. I would go further and call it a love crisis.

Why is this? Why is it so difficult to understand and practice love? Most people want to be loved and to love others, but we fail at this often. No one would argue that everyone needs love, yet its meaning can seem elusive and its practice so inconsistent.

In 1980, the country singer Johnny Lee wrote the song "Looking for Love." He opined over his failure to find love. He attributed his dilemma to the fact that he was "looking for love in all the wrong places." It makes the point that we can be mistaken about what love means and where to find it. So, perhaps the first question we should ask ourselves is where are we looking for it? Like our search for truth, what is the source we're using to understand what love means? Given the vast differences between definitions, they all can't be right.

If God is the author of love, He is the one qualified to define it. In the context of the structure and application of our faith, the materials that make up the leg of love must have integrity and proven dependability. And like our search for truth, understanding genuine love is found by way of its source. And it's necessary to understand this before it can be pursued and practiced.

Scriptures emphatically convey that God is love. It is an overwhelmingly significant part of His essence. And from one end of the Bible to the other, He clearly defines every aspect of love and what it should mean to us. Given all the misconceptions about love that inundate our culture, it is vital to our faith that we take the time to study and learn what God intended love to mean. And when we study what He says love is, we find some things that stand out about what genuine love looks like.

1. Love as God defines it is a choice.

Each of us has the capacity and responsibility to make meaningful choices. The most important ones involve those that define our character. Our character is molded and determined by whom and what we value, worship, and serve. Joshua made this clear to Israel when he confronted the elders, leaders, judges, and officials with a choice.

> Now fear the Lord and serve him with all faithfulness. Throw away the gods your ancestors worshiped beyond the Euphrates River and in Egypt, and serve the Lord. But if serving the Lord seems undesirable to you, then choose for yourselves this day whom you will serve, whether the gods your ancestors served beyond the Euphrates, or the gods of the Amorites, in whose land you are living.

> But as for me and my household, we will serve the
> Lord. (Joshua 24:14–15)

God has placed this choice before each of us. Choosing God's way is a choice to love.

Scriptures make something very clear about God's love for us: *nothing can separate us from it.*[2] This is a reality because He has chosen to make it so. He wants us to make the same choice to love so unconditionally that nothing can separate others from our love. I often must impress this upon my mind because choosing to love is not something I always want to do. I must bring my thoughts into submission to God and choose His standards for the way I love.

> A new commandment I give to you, that you love
> one another: just as I have loved you, you also are
> to love one another. (John 13:34)

Jesus's choice to love was not based upon whether He wanted to. He was tempted in all ways as we are, yet without sin.[3] He was certainly tempted to choose not to love. Every day and with every person, we have that same choice. If we had no choice in the matter, there would be no need for God to command us to do it! The choice before us is: Will it be His way or something else?

The culture we live in does not value love to the degree that God does and rarely condemns us for not choosing to love those it deems unworthy. The character traits of love such as empathy, forgiveness, patience, and mercy are often considered weaknesses. Our human nature can place requirements on love that mistakenly justify the choice not to love. Loving like Christ did insists that our love for others is consistent toward all people.[4] Like the choice Joshua put before Israel, whom do we choose to follow and serve?

God wants us to make the intentional decision to love.

2. Love as God defines it is authenticated by our behavior toward others.

Another way to put this is that our love for God is reflected in how we treat people. Because love is something we *do*. God equates loving Him with loving people. But loving others can be one of the most challenging, exasperating, and confrontational exercises of our will. It's easy to love God; He's perfect. Loving people? Not so much! Yet, our behavior toward others reveals the sincerity of our love for God, and we pass or fail the litmus test for the authenticity of our love for Him based upon how we treat others.[5]

> Little children, let us not love in word or talk but in
> deed and in truth. (1 John 3:18)

Loving deeds require truth, and truth resides in our thoughts. Our behavior toward people is framed by how we choose to think about them. I had to face up to this recently while working on a project in a large city. It necessitated my staying at a nearby hotel for weeks at a time. Every morning around six o'clock, I would walk five blocks from my hotel to the project. During this walk I would encounter dozens of people sleeping in doorways and on steam grates. Some were alone, and some slept in groups. Many were without a blanket or covering. Some had passed out on the sidewalk and were lying in their urine. My first reaction to this experience was revulsion toward and condemnation of them. How could they allow themselves to wind up in this situation? Had they no self-respect or dignity? They must be lazy and devoid of character.

But one morning before I left for work, my young grandchildren came to mind, and it dawned on me that these individuals were once like them—joyfully playing without a care in the world, excited about the possibilities that each new day might bring, and with all of life ahead of them. How then did the lives of these destitute people devolve to such a desperate condition?

The answer to that is complex, and it wasn't the lesson I needed to learn. I needed to understand that to treat people in a godly way I had to first think of them in a godly way. I was mortified by how far I was from doing this. I asked God to forgive me for my insensitivity and sense of superiority. I spent some time in the scriptures, bringing my thoughts to what they say about His love.[6] My hardheartedness toward them began to dissolve, and their situation became heartbreaking. From then on, I decided to help some of them with some of their physical needs, and I prayed for God to tend to them.

The point of this story is not about me. It's about the way we think about people. Because the way we think about them will eventually determine how we treat them.

We should remind ourselves that there was a time of desolation in each of our lives that levels the playing field for our opinion of others.

> As for you, you were dead in your transgressions and sins, in which you used to live when you followed the ways of this world and of the ruler of the kingdom of the air, the spirit who is now at work in those who are disobedient. All of us also lived among them at one time, gratifying the cravings of our flesh and following its desires and thoughts. Like the rest, we were by nature deserving of wrath. But because of his great love for us, God, who is rich in mercy, made us alive with Christ even when we were dead in transgressions—it is by grace you have been saved. (Ephesians 2:1–5)

We should be so thankful for God's mercy and grace that has brought us from death to life. If it weren't for Him, we would all be sleeping on a steam grate spiritually, and some of us, literally. Every life has a story, a history, and different events that have affected their current circumstances. But there is one constant about every life, one truth that puts loving others in its proper context: *Every human being is valuable to God.*[7] Because of this, we should respect every life. Jesus knew this and implored us to live this way.[8]

Additionally, how we behave toward people is continuously challenged. Not only toward those in the church, but in the neighborhood, with casual acquaintances, at work, and everyday encounters. Some people love us, some hate us, and others are indifferent toward us. But how they behave toward us is not the standard for how we are to treat them. If we are going to treat people in the way Jesus did, we first must take an honest look at how we think about people—all people. When the love of God constrains our thoughts, the loving way to act toward others will be apparent to us.

3.   Love as God defines it is unconditional.

Embedded in the DNA of love are the traits of forgiveness, mercy, grace, empathy, patience, and selflessness. These reflect the unconditional qualities of genuine love.[9] How contrary and exceptional this is compared to the provisional and restrictive measures we can place on whom we show our love!

"You can show love to someone without having much of a relationship. For example, the Good Samaritan in Luke 10:25–37 showed love to the wounded Jewish man, but he didn't even know him. He left him in the care of another even though he paid for the care. That is real love, and Jesus commends it."

John Piper

Often, we only love those whom we know well or deem worthy

of our love, and we can require an appreciative response to it. But those restrictions are not the pattern God has given us for genuine love. God loved and continues to love us even when we behave as if He is our enemy. Genuine love requires that our behavior reflects the same unconditional measure.[10]

4. Love as God defines it necessitates being involved with people.

I often say that it is easy to love everyone from our recliners. By that, I mean when we are isolated or insulated from others, the reality of what love requires is only in our imagination. We are not impacted or confronted by their difficult personalities, offended by what they say or do, exasperated by their politics and worldview, or challenged by their indifference to the needs of others. Perhaps God has placed people that are difficult to love in our lives because we need to learn to love them just as much as they need our love! And not from a distance, but up close and personal.

Distancing ourselves from people can give us a false sense of safety from getting used or hurt. In his book *The Four Loves*, C. S. Lewis insightfully makes the point: "The only place outside Heaven where you can be perfectly safe from all the dangers and perturbations of love is Hell."

The phrase "skin in the game" was made famous by investor Warren Buffet and referred to situations where investors use their own money to buy stock in the company they are running. Love requires skin in the game. It requires investing in love by our participation.

What does this participation look like? I put this question before my congregation, and here are some of the responses:

Being willing to be self-sacrificing and putting others before ourselves

Rolling up your sleeves and helping people deal with difficult life situations

Forgiving others as often as needed and not focusing on people's past mistakes

Treating people the way Jesus did with grace, empathy, value, and personal humility

Not being critical, bossy, judgmental, or acting superior, but speaking kind and encouraging words

Keeping confidences and avoiding gossip

Being friendly and enjoyable to be around and not being thin-skinned, easily offended, or angered

Encouraging people with wholesome words and not being rude, vulgar, or boorish

Not rejoicing in evil or being jealous of others

Valuing each person's life equally

Constantly praying for others and asking if you can pray with them about a particular situation or need

Being patient with people and willing to listen

Having your honest words tempered with kindness

In the incident at the beginning of this chapter, my father's reflection of many of these traits proved he loved me. When it comes to the structure of faith, the leg of love is composed of deeds—also known as our behavior toward others.

5.   Love as God defines it is something we grow in.

I think most people want to love and choose to love. We love *love*! As followers of Christ, love should be our priority, and we should behave in the way love compels us. Yet, we often regret our thoughts, words, and behavior because they have fallen short of the standard of love that scriptures teach and that Jesus exemplified. I have sometimes been ashamed of the unloving way I have behaved toward the most important people in my life! Unloving behavior is an indication of spiritual immaturity.

> When I was a child, I talked like a child, I thought
> like a child, I reasoned like a child. When I became a
> man, I set aside childish ways. (1 Corinthians 13:11)

Immaturity is a characteristic of every child and is why we equate it with childishness. We don't expect children to be mature in all their behavior, but we do expect them to grow into it over time. Similarly, our Heavenly Father desires His children to mature in our capacity and faithful practice of love, and He provides the means for us to grow and mature in it.

To begin with, we need to be well-grounded in its meaning. Depending on the version, the word *love* is mentioned up to 550 times in the Bible. It's important to immerse ourselves in the scriptural understanding of love.

For example, the Message Bible communicates some beautiful insight about growing in love.

> So this is my prayer: that your love will flourish and
> that you will not only love much but well. Learn to
> love appropriately. You need to use your head, and
> test your feelings so that your love is sincere and
> intelligent, not sentimental gush. Live a lover's life,
> circumspect and exemplary, a life Jesus will be proud
> of: bountiful in fruits from the soul, making Jesus
> Christ attractive to all, getting everyone involved in
> the glory and praise of God. (Philippians 1:9–11)

This translation is so rich in detail and content! It provides eleven measurable criteria for authentic and mature love. Like many of us do, I've made successive markings on my kitchen door frame as my children and grandchildren have grown taller. We should make time to evaluate how we are maturing in these spiritual "growth markings" of Christian love:

Our love should flourish.

We should love much and well.

We should love appropriately.

We must use our minds and reason to determine if our love is genuine.

We are to live love.

We must be circumspect (think before we do or say anything) about love.

We are to be examples of love.

We are to love in the way that Jesus would be proud of.

Our love should be fruitful.

Our love should make Jesus appealing to everyone.

Our love should inspire people to glorify and praise God.

The twentieth century British pastor John Henry Jowett challenged his readers in his expository *The Epistles of St. Peter* to grow in love with the following words:

> Push back the walls of family love until they include the neighbor; again, push back the walls until they include the stranger; again, push back the walls until they comprehend the foe.[11]

Jowett is making the point that as we mature in love, the perimeter of who we love should expand to include those we are close to and eventually embrace those who oppose us or might even do us harm. The ultimate example of this is God, who was willing to include the entire world in His ultimate loving sacrifice of His son to bring all people to Him.[12]

Growing in God's love is a lifelong pursuit and exercise. Apostle Paul encourages even those that love well to continue to grow in it.

We should never settle for being "loving enough." Instead, we should aspire to love more and more.

> Now about your love for one another, we do not need to write to you, for you yourselves have been taught by God to love each other. And in fact, you do love all of God's family throughout Macedonia. Yet we urge you, brothers and sisters, to do so more and more. (1 Thessalonians 4:9–10)

God has given us each other to learn from and put His love into practice. We mature in love as we love one another and expand our love to everyone.

> No one has ever seen God. If we love each other, God lives in us, and his love is perfected in us. (1 John 4:12)

Adam Clarke, the British Methodist theologian, defines this perfected love as having "achieved its full accomplishment, having molded us according to its own nature."[13]

Love as God defines it is a choice, is authenticated by behavior, is unconditional, involved in others' lives and is something He expects us to grow in.

THE PERSONIFICATION OF LOVE

The life of Jesus was love incarnate. The way Jesus loved epitomized selflessness, sacrifice, and, most importantly, a reflection of the character of God. His love is a gift to us, which He paid for with His life. We can't be good enough to earn it, and we can't be bad enough to lose it. As we study His life, we learn what love is and what it looks like when it is put into practice.

Jesus commanded us to love our neighbors as ourselves.[14] We need to give love, but how can we give something we don't have? Before we can give it, we also need to receive it. The unconditional nature of God's love is not only to be extended to others, but also toward ourselves!

Accepting God's unconditional love for you can be very difficult. That's usually because of the circumstances of our past. Perhaps you have done some things you consider unforgivable. You may have had erroneous religious teaching. You may have grown up in a family or under circumstances where love had to be earned, or it may have even been absent. But this is not the case with Christ. We don't earn it. It is not a response to something we did or didn't do. It's a personal gift from, freely given to us, and never taken back.

> Christ died for us while we were still sinners. This demonstrates God's love for us. (Romans 5:8)

Consider the truth that Christ's love for us was unconditional when we were separated from him and before we were brought into the new life He died to make available to us. Why would it then become conditional now that we are attempting to follow Him as our Lord?

When we look for and depend upon humanity for love, we can be disappointed. In contrast, we see this unconditional aspect of Christ's love when we look at whom He loved: doubters, those without faith, adulterers, prostitutes, the mentally ill, the homeless and needy, and the rich and powerful. In other words, He loved all of humanity. There were no conditions placed upon it, especially the requirement of expecting something in return for His love. In Christ, love can always be found. Romans chapter 8 assures us that nothing can ever separate us from God's love, which Christ shows us.[10] Nothing in this life, anything in creation, no force or power, and especially, nothing that we do or don't do can put a gap between us and Christ's love for us.

> And I pray that you, being rooted and established in love, may have power, together with all the Lord's holy people, to grasp how wide and long and high and deep is the love of Christ, and to know this love that surpasses knowledge—that you may be filled to the measure of all the fullness of God. (Ephesians 3:17–19)

Our very nature cherishes love above all else. We need to be convinced of God's unconditional and inseparable love for us. If you fill your thoughts with God's unconditional love for you, it will help you to share it unconditionally with others.

His love can be challenging for us to accept because it was so selfless and sacrificial.

> For God so loved the world, that he gave his only son, that whoever believes in him should not perish but have eternal life. (John 3:16 ESV)

Rarely does love challenge us to sacrifice our lives. But it can often challenge us to surrender our pride and self-centeredness, our time and resources, and the limits of our temperament, patience, and endurance. The leg of love is the most difficult to shape because it requires selflessness, and we are the last thing we want to give up! Philippians offers one of the most significant challenges we face regarding love.

> Do nothing out of selfish ambition or vain conceit. Rather, in humility value others above yourselves, not looking to your own interests but each of you

> to the interests of the others. In your relationships
> with one another, have the same mindset as Christ
> Jesus. (Philippians 2:3–5)

And this brings us to one of the most taxing aspects of loving like Christ: His love convicts us of what we "ought" to do.

I think that the word *ought* is one of the most remarkable words in the Bible. It's one of those words that can pierce our hearts about how we're living. And it's one of those words that strip us of the pretense and rationalization we often use to justify our self-centered behavior. The fact that we can consider and decide what we "ought" to do separates us from every other species. God challenges us about what we are doing with our entire life with this one word.

> What kind of people ought you to be? You ought to
> live holy and godly lives. (2 Peter 3:11)

What kind of people "ought" we be? Holy and godly. We move in that direction by answering a question that the well-known pastor Andy Stanley often asks during his sermons: "What does love require of me?" I believe that love defines what we "ought" to do. We're constantly faced with choices of what is the right, honest, fair, or wise thing to do. And while we have the freedom to do whatever we choose, as men and women professing godliness, we must dive a little deeper and ask: What does love require that we "ought" to do? If we can determine that, all those other questions are answered.

FAITH REQUIRES LOVE

> For [if we are] in Christ Jesus neither circumcision
> nor uncircumcision means anything, but only faith
> activated and expressed and working through love.
> (Galatians 5:6 AMP)

God has called all of humanity to receive wholeness, not because of the works that we do, or marked by any external sign such as circumcision, but by the finished work of salvation that Jesus accomplished. The important points are that salvation is not the end in itself but is the beginning of a life directed by faith, and the impressive power of love is not seen in what it is but in what it accomplishes.[15]

Why does faith require love? Love empowers our faith.

When it comes to shaping the leg of love as part of our faith, the important takeaway is this: The need to receive and give love is a foundational need of human existence. Choosing to love the way God defines it and in the way that Jesus lived it fulfills this need and empowers us to live in true freedom and peace.

CHAPTER 8

THE LEG OF FELLOWSHIP

Anyone who measures Christlikeness only in terms of growth in his or her fellowship with God takes an incomplete measurement. Spiritual maturity also includes growth in fellowship with the children of God.[1]

I have always loved family get-togethers. And from the time that I was a little child, into adolescence, and throughout adulthood, the Thanksgiving holiday has been one of the most enjoyable times for me. I loved having my entire family at our home, all seated around the table and enjoying a meal, having lively conversations, and hearing stories of what they had done since we had last all gotten together. When I got older and had a wife and daughter, Thanksgiving became even more important as our family expanded. The best time of all was when my daughter married and had children of her own, and we celebrated Thanksgiving with four generations of family.

But some things happened along the way that caused a gap in what I wanted Thanksgiving to be and what it became. Over time, my brothers and sister moved to opposite ends of the country to pursue their careers, my grandparents died, and my parents divorced and eventually passed away. Also, my wife and I moved to another state, and ultimately, my daughter, her husband, and two sweet grandchildren did the same.

Ironically, my daughter was born the day before Thanksgiving, and our first Thanksgiving meal with her was eaten in the hospital. For the next thirty-two years, we spent every Thanksgiving together. I'll never forget that first Thanksgiving my wife and I spent with just the two of us. We love each other dearly and are thankful to be in one another's lives every day. Despite this, we felt very alone.

We occasionally celebrate Thanksgiving together in recent years, but never as an entire family. We all call each other with Thanksgiving greetings and talk about what is going on in our lives and how we are each celebrating the holiday. And I wish that we were all present like we used to be. In the back of my mind, there is always that hollow and depressing feeling of loneliness because we are not together. I know they feel that way too. There is no substitute for being with those you love at a time or place that you value. And those times we can get together with family on Thanksgiving, or any time of year, are treasured.

But unlike me, who experiences loneliness a small handful of times a year, some people live in isolated and debilitating loneliness every day. According to the AARP, about one-third of US adults forty-five and older report feeling lonely. They have found that the population of lonely people over forty-five has grown by five million in the past eight years.[2]

Beyond the sad feelings it evokes, prolonged loneliness has been found to contribute to poor emotional and physical health. A well-known study performed in Alameda County, California[2] in 2010 found that the chances of all-cause mortality were significantly higher among respondents who often feel lonely than those who report that they never feel lonely. The internationally peer-reviewed journal *Heart* suggests that deficiencies in social relationships are associated with an increased risk of developing cardiac health disease and stroke.[3]

Current psychological research identifies two categories of loneliness. One is called social and emotional loneliness, and the other is referred to as existential loneliness.

Social and emotional loneliness has been defined as "the unpleasant experience that occurs when a person's network of social relations is deficient in some important way, either quantitatively or qualitatively."[4] Social and emotional loneliness is associated with a lack of meaningful social relationships and a lack of social companionship. In acute cases, it can lead to harmful behaviors such as substance abuse and the hollow satisfaction of pornography and prostitution to experience a sense of connection. Children who grow up under these circumstances often become desperate for attention and acceptance in their teen years and are prone to be more susceptible to peer pressure, sexual promiscuity, association with gangs, and other socially dysfunctional groups to feel accepted. It's very prevalent among older adults who live alone and are disconnected from family and friends. Many live with depression and sadness because of it.[5]

Existential loneliness is even more insidious. It is defined as "an intolerable emptiness, sadness, and longing that results from the awareness of one's fundamental separateness as a human being." Existential loneliness results from a broader separation related to the nature of existence and, in particular, a lack of meaning in life. An individual may even be in the company of others but experience existential loneliness. Additionally, mortality-related fears were associated with this type of loneliness, including the fear of disappearing from the earth, the fear of being forgotten, and the fear of dying. It's the kind of loneliness that hides behind the smile, lurks beneath the surface of self-confidence, diminishes the value of personal success, and slowly numbs the enjoyment of friendships.

Researchers in the sociological and related fields have found that social and emotional loneliness can be overcome by improving the quality of the network of relationships or by adjusting the level of hope or ambition of achieving something. On the other hand, existential loneliness is considered to have no known permanent remedy.[6]

The fear of rejection is deeply woven into the matrix of loneliness, whether social, emotional, or existential. It's that feeling that we are in some way inadequate, somehow deficient in some way. We can compare our intelligence, social skills, physical attractiveness, education, financial resources, and importance in the culture to others and conclude that we have little significance. It is a powerful fear that often has a far-reaching impact on our lives. Most people experience some anxiety when placing themselves in situations that could lead to rejection, but the fear becomes crippling for some people. An untreated fear of rejection may worsen over time, leading to greater and greater limitations in a sufferer's life.

Christians are not immune to any of this. Our significance in the body of Christ can appear minimal—that our sins are so egregious or habitual that we are unforgivable and that God is more interested in others who are less "damaged goods." We can question and even convince ourselves that we are less than God says we are.

There were times in my life when I felt that if people, especially those in the church, knew about my fears, shortcomings, weaknesses, and chronic sins, I would be rejected. Some of these insecurities went as far as to influence my relationship with my wife, as I feared she would leave or abandon me if I confessed these things to her. I felt like I had two versions of myself. The one on the outside exuded confidence and strength, and the one on the inside was weak, cowardly, and full of condemnation and guilt. The result was that I felt alone and isolated in the little world of who I really was.

When we allow these debilitating ideas to define our self-image and shape our relationships, the outcome is always the same. We isolate ourselves from and avoid participating, either physically or emotionally, in meaningful and fulfilling relationships outside and within the church. Sometimes even from God Himself. We wind up living in the lonely place where this separation leads us.

The point of this rather sobering introduction to this chapter is twofold. The first is to illustrate that the need for a sense of belonging, relationships based upon unconditional love and acceptance, and confidence in the makeup of our relationships is a deep and systemic need for every human being. As author and counselor Lily Fairchilde remarked:

> Deep down, even the most hardened criminal is starving for the same thing that motivates the innocent baby: love and acceptance.[7]

The second point is to demonstrate the gap between this need for connection and the consequences commonly experienced when it is compromised or nonexistent. The next chapter on the faith disciplines concerns narrowing and even closing that gap. The rest of this chapter is about what God intended relationships to be and what they should look like.

GOD IS ALL ABOUT RELATIONSHIP

One of the defining attributes of the nature of our God is that He is good. "God is good—All the time" is a popular phrase that has resonated throughout the church for decades. It is often used in a "call-and-response" pattern during the worship service. The idea that God is good all the time is expressed throughout the scriptures, and His goodness is seen in numerous ways. Many of David's prayers in the Psalms beautifully reflect this.

> For you, O Lord, are good and forgiving, abounding in steadfast love to all who call upon you. (Psalm 86:5 ESV)

> Praise the Lord! Oh give thanks to the Lord, for
> he is good, for his steadfast love endures forever!
> (Psalm 106:1 ESV)

> Praise the Lord, for the Lord is good; sing to his
> name, for it is pleasant! (Psalm 135:3 ESV)

Because God is good, He likes things that are good. And because He is good, He does not like things that are not good. And God has a lot to say about both. But in the context of this chapter, I want us to explore one thing that He says is not good. It's the *first* thing He says is not good, which emphasizes its importance to Him and should also for us. And it has significant relevance to faith.

> The Lord God said, "It is not good for the man to
> be alone." (Genesis 2:18)

The context here is that of God providing a woman for man to be his partner, but the point is God's desire for people to be in a relationship. It's one of the very first issues God addresses for humankind. The importance of this to God cannot be overstated. The essence of even God Himself is expressed in the eternal relationship between the Father, the Son, and the Holy Spirit. In fact, one of the overriding themes of the Bible, from Genesis through Revelation, is that of relationship.

Starting with the creation of man in Genesis, through the laws of the Old Testament, the good news of the Gospels, the formation and function of Christ's church, to the return of Christ and the eternal union of all believers with Christ and God, relationship is at the center of and purpose behind God's plan. And the focus throughout this magnificent, sometimes tragic, often heartbreaking, but always compelling drama is the relationship between God and people and our relationship with one another.

When Adam and Eve disobeyed God in the Garden of Eden, the primary and tragic consequence was that it permanently injured their relationship with God. Before this, they were open to God about everything. Their lives were entirely transparent to Him. There was no fear in their lives, and they had no doubt or guilt as they communed with Him. Their relationship with Him was honest and pure. After their sin, their relationship took a dramatic turn. Instead of desiring His presence, they hid from Him. They made clothing because their self-image had changed from being acceptable to God to feeling unworthy and vulnerable. There was now a gap between what their relationship with God could and should be and what it had become.

Imagine your children feeling so unworthy of your love and unacceptable to you that they would hide from your presence. Like you, this would have been heartbreaking to God. Humankind has always been God's portion.[8] In other words, we are what He gets, and His great desire is for us to seek out a relationship with Him. Apostle Paul makes this point passionately to his audience at Mars Hill in Athens.

> The God who made the world and everything in it is the Lord of heaven and earth and does not live in temples built by human hands. And he is not served by human hands, as if he needed anything. Rather, he himself gives everyone life and breath and everything else. From one man he made all the nations, that they should inhabit the whole earth, and he marked out their appointed times in history and the boundaries of their lands. God did this so that they would seek him and perhaps reach out for him and find him, though he is not far from any one of us. For in him we live and move and have our

being. As some of your own poets have said, "We are his offspring." (Acts 17:24–28)

God has always desired His creation to be in a relationship with Him and one another. He never intended for us to be alone. When we look into His Word and understand His purposes and plans for humankind, we see that God wants us to understand the significance of relationship to the point that it becomes our passion.

VALIDATING RELATIONSHIP

When I consider that God does not want me to be alone but to be in relationships, the first question that comes to mind is, why? What is it about relationships that God considers suitable? What is their purpose, and why are they essential to faith?

I believe the answers to those questions are found in understanding and participating in a specific aspect of a relationship that sets it apart from simply knowing or being acquainted with someone. *Relationship* is a broad term. We're in a relationship with everyone we meet, no matter how briefly or under what circumstances. But the kind of relationship that God desires for us to have with our Christian brothers and sisters, especially with Him, is much deeper than that. It's not only more personal and meaningful, but it's also transparent in its honesty, it's selfless in its love, it's transformative in its effect, and it's covenantal in its commitment. It's an essential requirement for Christlike faith.

It's called fellowship.

In the New Testament, fellowship can be defined as: our intentional and knowledgeable agreement on what God has done through Christ that we live out with Him and together in harmonious community.

Fellowship nurtures a transformational depth of intimacy,

honesty, and trust in our relationship with God and Jesus. Because of that, it evokes a loving and trusting allegiance and camaraderie between those who follow Jesus.

The concept of fellowship is beautifully conveyed by apostle John in his first epistle:

> That which was from the beginning, which we have heard, which we have seen with our own eyes, which we have gazed upon and touched with our own hands—this is the Word of life. And this is the life that was revealed; we have seen it and testified to it, and we proclaim to you the eternal life that was with the Father and was revealed to us. We proclaim to you what we have seen and heard, so that you also may have fellowship with us. And this fellowship of ours is with the Father and with His Son, Jesus Christ. We write these things so that our joy may be complete. (1 John 1:1–4)

The fellowship spoken of here is with God, Jesus, and the apostles. And if we have fellowship with them, we have fellowship with each other. But the central theme and binding material of our fellowship is the Word of life, Jesus Christ. Through this Word of life, the living Word of God, we are brought to an understanding and experience of what fellowship means and requires. As we live in fellowship with God's Word, we live in fellowship with God, Jesus, and one another. And when we do, we receive the fullness of joy that this fellowship provides.

These attributes of fellowship run contrary to the characteristics of the secular culture and our human nature. We like having relationships, but we don't like the requirements they place on us. We want relationships that we have control over and that we can walk away from when they don't meet our expectations. We like relationships that benefit us but don't require much of us in return. It sounds selfish, and shallow, doesn't it? And in the church, and especially with Him, God wants us to avoid relationships like this.[10] They are not the way He intended our relationship with Him or other Christians to be. He wants our relationship with Him and our brothers and sisters in Christ to be rich, intimate, compassionate, trustworthy, sacrificial, and edifying.

FAITH REQUIRES FELLOWSHIP WITH THE SPIRIT OF GOD

Genuine faith requires that God is recognizably active in our lives as the Father, the Son, and the Holy Spirit. For this to happen, we must arrive at a place of humility and surrender to God. We place nothing ahead of or in front of our relationship with Him. We are in fellowship with His purposes, plans, and values. This enables us to connect with the divine nature of Christ in a profoundly personal way and have unity and communion with Christ and the Holy Spirit. That makes our faith more than a word or idea. It makes it real. It becomes transformative. When our relationship with Him is that of fellowship, we experience the active engagement of God, Jesus, and the Holy Spirit in our faith.

> I pray that out of his glorious riches, he may strengthen you with power through his spirit in your inner being, so that Christ may dwell in your hearts through faith. (Ephesians 3:16–17)

As the Spirit of God becomes recognizably active in our lives through our fellowship with Him, our faith journey is powerfully refreshed each day. There is no obstacle, circumstance, human limitation, or personal weakness that we cannot overcome. The next chapter on the faith disciplines explains the method that God has given us for deepening our fellowship with Him.

Faith is, at its nucleus, a deeply spiritual matter. It requires our fellowship with God, who is a spiritual being. In the absence of His Spirit, it is impossible to understand, much less live by.[10]

FAITH REQUIRES FELLOWSHIP
WITH THE PEOPLE OF GOD

It has taken me some time to recognize and value the relevance of fellowship with the church to faith. The beginnings of my faith journey had always been so focused on my relationship with God that I missed seeing that He never intended for me to be on it without other like-minded people. And honestly, I wanted to be on it without them. Relationships, including even those within the family of God, can be messy, stressful, and demanding. Like the challenge to love unconditionally, it was one thing for me to have fellowship with a perfect being. It was quite another to have it with imperfect, flawed human beings like myself! But as I grew in my desire to be a committed follower of Jesus, His words about true discipleship convicted me.

> A new command I give you: Love one another. As
> I have loved you, so you must love one another. By
> this everyone will know that you are my disciples,
> if you love one another. (John 13:34–35)

Loving people requires knowing people, knowing people requires spending time with them, and having fellowship with people requires all three. How could I be a true disciple, and how would anyone know I was if I was not actively involved in loving relationships with people? As I have gotten further along this faith path, I have come to realize that God has called us to love each other for a reason. And the primary reason is that it is how we learn to fellowship with each other.[11]

It's easy to *say* we have fellowship with people when we don't really know them! When we're not intentionally engaged in building relationships, we don't have to deal with one another's failures, weaknesses, selfish behavior, and attitudes. Fellowship requires that we engage with one another, depend on each other to do what we say we will, work through difficult circumstances and disagreements, worship and serve together with a like-minded purpose, and help each other overcome our character flaws. And these are precisely the challenges that God knows we need to work through to learn to have fellowship together.[12]

Jesus also prioritizes maintaining our fellowship with each other that we ought to take very seriously.

> Therefore, if you are offering your gift at the altar and there remember that your brother or sister has something against you, leave your gift there in front of the altar. First go and be reconciled to them; then come and offer your gift. (Matthew 5:23–24)

I wonder how much smaller our worship services would be if we practiced this! But seriously, how can we sit there and worship in genuine fellowship with God when we have broken fellowship with believers, perhaps even sitting in the same room with us? What is the priority that Jesus is making here?

> But if we say we love God and don't love each other, we are liars. We cannot see God. So how can we love God, if we don't love the people we can see? (1 John 4:20)

Our fellowship with each other requires mutual humility and accountability. There is no room for divisions, judgment, condescension, or hurtful behavior. If and when it happens, we are to restore the relationship quickly and not let things fester.[13]

As we read in apostle John's first epistle, fellowship brings joy. If joy is lacking in our relationships, it's because our fellowship with God or one another is lacking somehow. Jesus's teachings and those of the apostles identify what fellowship in Christ's church looks like. The measure to which the qualities listed here are evident with our brothers and sisters gives us a window into how genuine it is:

Treating one another with love, respect, selflessness, and kindness

Encouraging and building one another up with the Word of God

Trusting one another to keep confidences

Being generous with our material resources

Being aware of the needs of others and willing to help

Partaking in each other's sufferings and troubles, as well as comfort and joy

We should ask ourselves if there are any gaps between these qualities of the genuine fellowship that God desires and the reality of what defines our relationships. If they exist, do you "offer your gift at the altar" while allowing them to continue? What are you going to do about it?

TREASURING FELLOWSHIP

In the antique world, the worth of a chair or any object is based on multiple values. These values are determined by its rarity, artistic merit and beauty, the history of who has owned it, how it has been used, its overall condition, and numerous other factors. These values are prized by collectors and often result in competition for owning them that can drive their prices to extremes.

In our relationships with God and one another, we must understand their worth and treasure their values. And when we remove the trappings and distractions of materialism, our accomplishments, our focus on how "important" we are, and get down to what is worth something, isn't what makes our lives truly rich the value of our relationships?

The value of our fellowship with God and one another recorded in Paul's letter to the Ephesians beautifully expresses what a treasure these relationships contain.

Praise the God and Father of our Lord Jesus Christ! Through Christ, God has blessed us with every spiritual blessing that heaven offers. Before creating the world, he chose us through Christ to be holy and perfect in his presence. Because of his love, He had already decided to adopt us through Jesus Christ. He freely chose to do this so that the kindness he had given us in his dear Son would be praised and given glory.

Through the blood of his Son, we are set free from our sins. God forgives our failures because of his overflowing kindness. He poured out his kindness by giving us wisdom and insight of his plan for us. He decided to do this through Christ. He planned to bring all of history to its goal in Christ. Then Christ would be the head of everything in heaven and on earth. God also decided ahead of time to choose us through Christ according to His plan, which makes everything work the way He intends.

> He planned all of this so that we would praise Him and give Him glory. You heard and believed the message of truth, the Good News that He has saved you. In Him, you were sealed with the Holy Spirit whom He promised. This Holy Spirit is the guarantee that we will receive our inheritance. We have this guarantee until we are set free to belong

to Him. God receives praise and glory for this.
(Ephesians 1:3–14 GWT)

Have you ever considered *why* you value your relationship with
God and His church? Why not take some time and write down some
reasons why you do. It will help you treasure them.

THE PERSONIFICATION OF FELLOWSHIP

The entirety of Jesus's life and ministry was about relationships.
Jesus's prayer in John chapter 17 illustrates how precious our
fellowship is to God, with Him, and with each other. In this prayer,
He makes four points that we should cherish:

Jesus made known and exemplified that our relationship with
God is that of a loving, forgiving, and protective Father to His
family.

Jesus made known and exemplified that He was the way into
this relationship and that it can be intimate and transformative.

Jesus made known and exemplified that our relationship with
each other reflects the depth and genuine quality of our love for and
relationship with God.

Jesus made known and exemplified that our relationship with
humankind is a witness to God's existence, truth, love, and calling
for all people.

Would we all follow His example!

SEATED AT THE TABLE OF FELLOWSHIP

Imagine yourself seated at an enormous banquet table with hundreds
of people. All those sitting at the table are unique in their personality,
interests, nationality, education, and ethnicity. Even though many
of the guests have never met before, a bond of love is reflected in the

joyful, engaging, and edifying conversations. Everyone genuinely cares for the people around them and treats them like family. They speak into one another's lives with loving and humble honesty, and wise counsel can be heard in some dialogue. Forgiveness is asked for and given freely when it is needed.

Despite all the differences that are evident among the guests at this banquet, two essential commonalities powerfully unify the relationship of those present.

First, at the head of the table sits Jesus Christ. He has invited every guest, not just as an acquaintance but as a family member. Everyone there acknowledges Jesus as the host and why they have been invited. Each guest has formed a deep and abiding trust and worship of the Father, Son, and Holy Spirit. Because of this, there is humble acknowledgment of, and thankfulness for God's presence reflected in how they value each other that brings unity and harmony to their fellowship.

Second, each of the chairs they are seated in, while unique in its appearance, has a trustworthy base that securely supports the weight and individual characteristics of the life seated upon it. It's a base designed and built with the materials of genuine, godly faith. A faith that recognizes the equal value of all guests to the host and therefore to each other.

This is a picture of what genuine fellowship looks like.

> Instead, speaking the truth in love, we will grow to become in every respect the mature body of him who is the head, that is, Christ. From him the whole body, joined and held together by every supporting ligament, grows and builds itself up in love, as each part does its work. (Ephesians 4:15–16)

Fellowship is a covenantal relationship with God and one another. Faith requires both.

The strength, love, acceptance, and transformative power of relationship are only found in its most intimate dimension, that of fellowship. God created this earth so that it would sustain human life. Human life that was created in His image and for the purpose of fellowship with Him and each other. The sobering and incredible reality that we can have fellowship with Almighty God, the creator of the universe, the being that made us and knows us individually and intimately, should arrest our attention, rearrange our every priority, and become the passion of our lives. The fellowship we have with one another should be shaped by pointing us to that fellowship with God. God has set the wheels of history and destiny in motion with the purpose of relationships that glorify Him.[14] These relationships are framed by God's truth, bathed in His love, and nurtured by fellowship.

We have looked at aspects of relationship that reveal its deeply ingrained human need, purpose and value to God, vital role in the church, and relevance to faith. There will always be more to learn, but most importantly, to practice. And if I could convince you of one thing to do with resolve from what has been written here, it would be this: Watch over and care for your fellowship with God and His church in the same way you watch over and care for your life. Your faith cannot support your life without it.

CHAPTER 9

THE LEG OF FAITH DISCIPLINES

Translate your dreams of spiritual growth into concrete patterns of behavior that God has designed to promote your spiritual progress.

—*R. C. Sproul*

For several years I practiced martial arts. Like many others, my interest in it began when I watched Bruce Lee in the movie *Enter the Dragon*. His physical appearance, strength, grace, speed, and flexibility impressed a picture upon me of what I would like to become. I wanted the self-confidence and security that He personified. It wasn't until I was in my mid-thirties that I began to train in martial arts. Little did I know that Lee started his study of martial arts in his early teens and trained every day of his entire life. It occupied most of his day, and it became the driving force of his life, while it was basically just a hobby for me. Still, I was convinced that by attending two classes a week and practicing my forms, I could transform myself from a rather clumsy, inflexible martial arts neophyte into the picture of an athletic, feared, and formidable opponent within a few years.

After beginning to learn and practice the various forms and

immerse myself in the exercises, I understood the level of effort and commitment required to get to the place I had pictured. Even though I was involved with martial arts for the next fifteen years, I didn't get to the level of proficiency that I initially wanted to. Why? I decided that I wasn't willing to give it the priority of time and practice that was needed. So, I lowered my expectations and settled for what I considered to be "good enough."

I wonder how often we do this with our spiritual life?

We may be passionate about being firmly grounded in the truth, yearn to love like Jesus did, and desire a deep and abiding fellowship with God and His church. These are honorable and godly intentions, and without them, we would never even begin a faith journey. But faith is not a gift. It is, at its core, a relationship.[1] And, like all relationships, it involves effort on the part of both parties. We know God's effort to know us,[1] to draw us to Him and equip us with what we need to *become* people of great faith and godliness. But what effort are *we* willing to make in this relationship? Are we willing to do the work that an intimate and engaged fellowship with God and His people requires, or would we rather lower our expectations and settle for "good enough"?

On our journey of faith, the path that God has laid out for us is often easy—the trail is flat, the view is stunning, the day is beautiful, and we feel great. At other times, the path becomes difficult, and the route can become increasingly steep, requiring more effort. We can feel as if our progress is minimal during those times and not be so enthusiastic about the journey! Storms of ignorance can cloud our view, and we can be confronted with obstacles of doubt, fear, apathy, and self-centeredness. We can be under attack from predators trying to pull us off the path through deception, mockery, and vitriol.

When we look at Bruce Lees of faith in the Bible, in history, or perhaps ones we know, we see similar characteristics. They take their God-given abilities and use them with intention and consistency as committed athletes. They never settle for "good enough."

Instead, they know where they are going and are consummately dedicated to getting there. They train every day, are grounded in the fundamentals, and always strive to improve. When obstacles appear, they do what they must to overcome them and seek out help when necessary. They don't allow the godly words they choose to define themselves to be overshadowed with terms of defeat. Apostle Paul, through his Spirit-inspired words, uses an athletic analogy to teach us about perseverance in one of his letters to the Corinthians.

> Don't you realize that everyone who runs in a race runs to win, but only one runner gets the prize? Run like them so that you can win. Everyone who enters an athletic contest goes into strict training. They do it to win a temporary crown, but we do it to win one that will be permanent. So, I run, but not without a clear goal ahead of me. So, I box, but not as if I were just shadow boxing. Rather, I toughen my body with punches and make it my slave so that I will not be disqualified after I have spread the Good News to others. (1 Corinthians 9:24–27)

Progress along the path of our journey of faith requires no less. And the rewards for our faithful efforts are far more consequential than any prize in the physical realm.

> Be doers of the Word, and not hearers only. Otherwise, you are deceiving yourselves. Anyone who hears the Word but does not carry it out is like a man who looks at his face in a mirror, and after observing himself, he goes away and immediately forgets what he looks like. But the one who looks intently into the perfect law of freedom and continues to do so, not being a forgetful hearer, but

an effective doer, he will be blessed in what he does. (James 1:22–25)

God is certainly willing to help us on that journey in a powerful and personal way. In the person of Jesus Christ, it is a journey that He walks along with us with every step. But He is not going to make that journey for us. He expects us to use what He has given us in His Word and His Spirit and do something with it. Apostle Peter speaks to this in his second letter.

> His divine power has given us everything we need for life and godliness through the knowledge of Him who called us by His own glory and excellence. Through these He has given us His precious and magnificent promises, so that through them you may become partakers of the divine nature, now that you have escaped the corruption in the world caused by evil desires. (2 Peter 1:3–4)

Peter goes on to make the point that, like any relationship, our relationship with God can deepen, be strengthened, and mature to the end of fellowship. Still, it requires identifiable effort and faithful, consistent practice.

> For this very reason, make every effort to add to your faith, goodness; and to goodness, knowledge; and to knowledge, self-control; and to self-control, perseverance; and to perseverance, godliness; and to godliness, mutual affection; and to mutual affection, love. For if you possess these qualities in increasing measure, they will keep you from being ineffective and unproductive in your knowledge of our Lord Jesus Christ. (2 Peter 1:5–8)

The word *add* in verse 5 might seem to imply that the list of character qualities that follow are separate from or in addition to our faith, but this is not the case. The original word expresses the idea that they are part of faith and that Paul is singling them out so that we understand them as necessary components of faith. He wants us to persevere in developing them. As we grow in them, we receive the fruits of our labor, or as the Good News Translation puts it, "they will make you active and effective in your knowledge of our Lord Jesus Christ."

VALIDATING THE DISCIPLINES

God wants the truth He has given us to produce fruit, benefits, and blessings. He wants us to enter that Promised Land of Godliness. But He requires a lot of us for that to happen. He points out in these verses that we are responsible for building these and other qualities into our faith. So, the question becomes, how do we do that?

> All Scripture is God-breathed and is useful for teaching, rebuking, correcting and training in righteousness, so that the servant of God may be thoroughly equipped for every good work. (2 Timothy 3:16–17)

The equipment that scripture gives us to grow in godliness is what I call the faith disciplines. I define the faith disciplines as the spiritual exercises and practices that God has given us to build our faith.

Jesus summarized His Sermon on the Mount by comparing the *practice* of what He taught to that of the firm foundation of a house. He also puts the responsibility for that practice on us.

Therefore everyone who hears these words of mine and puts them into practice is like a wise man who built his house on the rock. The rain came down, the streams rose, and the winds blew and beat against that house; yet it did not fall, because it had its foundation on the rock. But everyone who hears these words of mine and does not put them into practice is like a foolish man who built his house on sand. The rain came down, the streams rose, and the winds blew and beat against that house, and it fell with a great crash. (Matthew 7:24–27)

Are you willing to try to follow the directions for that journey with the tools that God has given you? If so, you are on the path that Henry Varley inspired the world-famous evangelist Dwight Moody with something he never forgot, something far beyond a faith that is merely "good enough": "The world has yet to see what God can do with and for and through and in a man [or woman] who is fully and wholly consecrated to Him."[1]

Consecration is the solemn dedication to a particular purpose or service. The word *consecration* literally means "association with the sacred." That association is based on and deepens with the truth, love, fellowship, and mindfulness consistently put into practice in our lives. The faith disciplines define what efforts *we* are to make to live a consecrated life.

TRANSFORMATIONAL DISCIPLINE

As Christians, we talk a lot about transformation. We yearn to be transformed to live like Jesus:

We yearn to be close to God like He was and live the godly and fruitful life He said was available.

We strive to reflect His love for God and for people.

We endeavor to serve God intentionally and wholeheartedly like He did.

As part of this pursuit, we study and apply what is commonly referred to as the "spiritual disciplines" or "Christian disciplines." These are the practices or exercises that the Word of God gives us to "train ourselves to be godly," as 1 Timothy teaches:

> Have nothing to do with godless myths and old wives' tales; rather, train yourself to be godly. Physical training is good, but training for godliness is much better, promising benefits in this life and in the life to come. (1 Timothy 4:7)

As defined in chapter 1, godliness involves a profoundly intimate and meaningful relationship with God that dominates and governs every aspect of how we live. And the degree of godliness we experience is not only up to God. It is our responsibility also. Paul deliberately emphasized to Timothy that we've got to work at it. Dallas Willard corroborated this in *The Spirit of the Disciplines* when he made the point that, "we also learn by experience that the harmonization of our total self with God will not be done for us. *We* must act."[2]

So, the purpose of practicing these disciplines is to develop spiritual formation, growth, and maturity in our faith. They are how we become intentional in our pursuit of godliness, and they have a transformational impact on us. I refer to them as the "faith disciplines" because they are how we develop our faith and make it real to us. I like to think of them as "faith-building exercises." As we employ them, we develop habits that bring us into a deeper understanding and value of being obedient to God and into the realm of godliness. They cause us to connect with God and each other personally that cannot be achieved otherwise.

Dallas Willard speaks to this in the introduction to his book, *Renovation of the Heart*:

> Spiritual formation in Christ is an orderly process. Although God can triumph in disorder, that is not His choice. There is also needed an understanding of exactly what needs to be done and how it can be accomplished: of the instruments for the realization of that life and the order of their use.[3]

We must understand how the word *discipline* is used in the Bible rather than in its current vernacular usage. Today, when we consider the term *discipline*, we often equate it with the idea of punishment. A quick search of the meaning on the internet will provide the word's primary meaning as "the practice of training people to obey rules or a code of behavior, using punishment to correct disobedience." But this is not the word's primary meaning as it is used in the Bible. The *Holman Bible Dictionary* provides the original meaning:

> Discipline comes from the Latin word "disco," which means learning or getting to know, a direct kind of acquaintance with something or someone. Discipline refers to the process by which one learns a way of life. Such learning required a relationship between the master who knew the way of life (discipline) and a learner (a disciple). Within this relationship, the master led a learner through a process (the discipline) until the learner could imitate or live like the master. A disciple was like an apprentice learning a trade or craft from a master.
>
> Discipline, biblically understood, results in blessing. God's people learn how to serve Him. Through

praise and correction, their lives are shaped into a pattern of consistent obedience and love. Within "the discipline of the Lord," expressed in and through the Lord Jesus Christ, one can live the kind of life which is pleasing to God and of benefit to others.

At sixteen years of age, when I started an apprenticeship with a master furniture maker, one of the first things I learned was how to sharpen a wood chisel. My teacher showed me all the steps involved and then had me do them while he was watching. A little while later, I started changing the technique he showed me because I thought I had found a more effective way of sharpening the chisels than his. Once he was satisfied that I was doing what he showed me correctly, he went to do other things and left me on my own.

When he came back to check on my progress and asked why I wasn't doing what he told me, I said to him that I had found a better process. He told me that when I could get a chisel as sharp as possible by using his method, I could change and use my own, but not until then. I began to argue with him about this. His response of an ultimatum was not what I had anticipated. He made it crystal clear that if I did not follow his instructions, I could not be his apprentice.

His rebuke challenged my prideful ignorance. And at that moment, I realized that there were some requirements to being his apprentice that involved more than just showing up for work on time. I needed a different attitude—an attitude of obedience. So, I had a choice to make. I weighed the alternatives. I decided to obey his instructions because I valued being his student more than trying to learn the trade on my own or elsewhere.

Jesus established a master-learner relationship with His primary followers for them to become His disciples. Like my apprenticeship, as they lived and worked with Him, Jesus disciplined them in His understanding of what God wanted. Such discipline involved praise and criticism, affirmation and rebuke. The success of His mission depended on His training this small group of followers because they would carry on His work after His death and resurrection. The twelve were His apprentices in the work that God called Jesus to do. We are called to be His apprentices in discipleship for this same work, and we are commissioned to disciple others.

Like my apprenticeship, learning to be godly involves more than just showing up for activities. It requires an attitude of obedience and humility to the master, Jesus Christ. While our hypersensitive and me-centered culture is averse to criticism, even if it is constructive and deserved, Jesus's correction and sometimes rebuke are not punishment. It is part of the learning process to help us overcome attitudes that value our will and purposes over His. His discipline of us is rooted in His love and desire for us to become close to God.

Hebrews explains the purpose and value of godly discipline to faith. First, we are charged with looking to Jesus as our ultimate example of faith. In that context, God speaks about discipline because it is a prime ingredient in developing faith.

> In your struggle against sin, you have not yet resisted to the point of shedding your blood. And have you completely forgotten this Word of encouragement that addresses you as a father addresses his Son? It says, "My Son, do not make light of the Lord's discipline, and do not lose heart when he rebukes you, because the Lord disciplines the one he loves, and he chastens everyone he accepts as his Son." (Hebrews 12:4–11)

Endure hardship as discipline; God is treating you as His children. For what children are not disciplined by their father? If you are not disciplined—and everyone undergoes discipline—then you are not legitimate, not true sons and daughters at all. Moreover, we have all had human fathers who disciplined us, and we respected them for it. How much more should we submit to the Father of spirits and live! They disciplined us for a little while as they thought best; but God disciplines us for our good, so that we may share in His holiness. No discipline seems pleasant at the time, but painful. Later, however, it produces a harvest of righteousness and peace for those who have been trained by it.

God wants us to share in His holiness. Only our prideful ignorance can make His words seem difficult and even feel painful at times. But like having sore muscles after a rigorous workout at the gym, pain or discomfort can indicate that we are growing. As we intentionally put into practice what Jesus taught, we are strengthening the capabilities of our knowledge, our humility, our trust, and our surrender to our Lord. We are going through a transformation. We are building spiritual muscle! And the primary transformation that the faith disciplines develop and nurture is that of our heart. They produce that harvest of righteousness and peace that consecrated fellowship with God securely establishes.

FAITH REQUIRES DISCIPLINE

Numerous books have been written on the practice of the spiritual or faith disciplines. They vary somewhat in the specific categories, but most focus on the "classical" disciplines. They are called classical because they are *central* to experiential Christianity and are considered necessary for intentional Christian life. For our purposes, we will look at their application of, relevance to, and impact on, their relationship with the other legs of truth, love, and fellowship that our faith is constructed of. Appendix 4 has a list of well-known authors with comprehensive studies of each discipline.

The leg of the faith disciplines is what brings the transformative aspects of love, truth, and fellowship into meaningful and powerful reality for us. The classical disciplines most commonly written about and practiced are listed below. You will notice that these activities land in two categories: those we practice alone and those we participate in with others. Our intentional journey of faith requires both:

<u>Individual</u>

Study

Prayer

Meditation

Solitude and Silence

Fasting

Confession

Stewardship/Simplicity

<u>Communal</u>

Submission/Guidance

Worship and Celebration

Fellowship

Service

Evangelizing/Mentoring

Confession

These disciplines help us build integrity and strength into the other legs that form our faith—truth, love, and fellowship.

THE RELEVANCE OF THE DISCIPLINES TO TRUTH, LOVE, AND FELLOWSHIP

The Leg of Truth

Etched into the original CIA building's main lobby wall is the phrase, "And ye shall know the truth, and the truth shall make you free." Several universities, including Johns Hopkins University, Ottawa University, and Southern Methodist University, use the Latin version of the quote, "veritas liberabit vos," as their motto. It has been made into posters, referenced in country-western love songs, parodied in movies, and proclaimed by various civil rights leaders.

In all these uses, the words *knowledge* or *information* could be substituted for the word *truth*. But the two cannot be conflated. The quote's author, Jesus Christ, had an entirely different meaning and purpose for making this statement. The way it has been taken out of the context that Jesus intended and the everyday secularization of its use has redirected Jesus's point of pursuing spiritual truth that builds faith in secular knowledge and education.

If you hold to my teaching, you are really my disciples.

> Then you will know the truth, and the truth will
> set you free. (John 8:31–32)

The words "hold to my teaching" are also translated as "abide in my word," "remain faithful to my teaching," "keep on obeying what I have said," and "live by what I say." Jesus goes on to say that then, you will know the truth, and it will set you free. The focus here is on faithfully *living* the truth he taught. To do that, we first must know and understand it.

As we read earlier in 2 Timothy 3:16–17, the study of scripture, or educating ourselves in God's truth, is the only way we thoroughly equip ourselves with the truth. The good news is that it is easier to learn how to study the Bible than it has ever been since it was written. We have the total of all the knowledge, study aids, commentaries, versions of the Bible, and translations at our fingertips through the internet and in bookstores. We need not feel inadequate or unqualified for the task. God has made our minds capable of learning His Word because that is how we come to know Him.

Never allow yourself to be convinced that you are incapable of meaningful study and understanding of the scriptures. Being well versed in the scriptures is not reserved for scholarly academics. God wants you to know Him personally, and He reveals Himself to you through His Word. Because of that, He has made you capable of learning it. It will take some time and effort to learn how to effectively study and understand the scriptures, and some simple but valuable methods can easily be found online.

The value of the intentional study of God's Word is crucial to genuine faith, and it is listed first in the personal disciplines because it causes us to understand the purpose and practice of all the others. Concerning the individual disciplines:

It provides us with direction and examples of how to pray.

It forms the framework of our meditations.

It is the still small voice in our times of solitude and silence.

It teaches us the purpose and right attitude about fasting.

It convicts us of the sin and error we need to confess.

It provides us with directions on stewarding what God has blessed us with.

It gives us a context for what we should value that simplifies our priorities and interests.

And for the communal disciplines, it explains how submission and guidance, not only from God but within the church, can help us avoid bad choices, correct our mistakes, encourage us in our times of doubt, and help us learn humility.

The focus of and joy in our worship and celebration together

The purpose and need for our relationship of fellowship with each other

The personal fulfillment of service for God's purposes and its importance to His kingdom

The need for and confidence in evangelizing and mentoring others to become disciples of Jesus

How our burdens are lifted from being able to share confidences with others

The leg of truth is initially "machined" by our persistent, disciplined, and intentional study of God's Word. It is more deeply, intimately, and distinctively shaped, smoothed, and beautifully polished by the other disciplines.

THE LEG OF LOVE

Love is something that is never spoken of negatively in the Bible. Scriptures never warn us of the problem of an abundance of love. Apostle Paul didn't write the believers in Corinth and say, "It's been reported that some individuals among you love people too much. This love thing has gotten out of hand. This needs to stop!" Scriptures do have a lot of negative things to say about being unloving. And the outcome or consequences of being unloving are very different than those of being loving.

When I was preparing for my wedding, I had to memorize my wedding vows to recite them when asked by the minister. Part of the vow was the promise to love my wife no matter the circumstance. While I was enthusiastic about and committed to the idea, I wondered how I would always fulfill this promise. I think this is because when I thought about love, I didn't think of being in control of it. I put it in the category of an emotional response rather than a learned behavior. This was made even more mystifying when I considered the idea of unconditional love. Yet, God not only wants us to love but to grow in it.

> Now about your love for one another we do not
> need to write to you, for you yourselves have been
> taught by God to love each other. And in fact, you
> do love all of God's family throughout Macedonia.
> Yet we urge you, brothers and sisters, to do so more
> and more. (1 Thessalonians 4:9–10)

We all understand this command to love. The question that needs answering is how do we do this and continue to grow in it? How does the leg of love become as supportive and dependable as Truth and Fellowship in our faith? I believe that the disciplines provide us with the avenue for this.

The individual disciplines provide clarity and understanding of what true love is. They humble us with the way God has unconditionally loved us through His Son, Jesus Christ.

As we:

study about God's meaning of love,

pray for His guidance and help,

meditate on the relevance of it,

fast over our vows to love,

examine our hearts and confess our sins when we fail to love,

spend time in solitude and silence,

and simplify our lives with God's priority to love.

Our hearts become convicted to love like He loves us. God can command us to love because He has given us the ability to love.

The more significant challenge to love often comes in the faithful practice of the communal disciplines. Here, the sincerity of our efforts in the individual disciplines is proven. It is here where our commitment to love is tested. *In these disciplines, our theory of love becomes our practice of love.*

The Message paraphrases John 4:20–21 in a way that makes this very clear.

> If anyone boasts, "I love God," and goes right on hating His brother or sister, He is a liar. If he won't love the person he can see, how can he love the God he can't see? The command we have from Christ is blunt: Loving God includes loving people. You've got to love both.

> The fourth chapter of Ephesians explains the unifying bond that loving our brothers and sisters brings to the interrelationship of truth and

fellowship to love. It is a bond that cannot happen without the communal disciplines.

Be completely humble and gentle; be patient, bearing with one another in love. Make every effort to keep the unity of the Spirit through the bond of peace. There is one body and one Spirit, just as you were called to one hope when you were called; one Lord, one faith, one baptism; one God and Father of all, who is over all and through all and in all. (Ephesians 4:2–6)

So, Christ Himself gave the apostles, the prophets, the evangelists, the pastors, and teachers, to equip His people for works of service, so that the body of Christ may be built up until we all reach unity in the faith and in the knowledge of the Son of God and become mature, attaining to the whole measure of the fullness of Christ. Then we will no longer be infants, tossed back and forth by the waves, and blown here and there by every wind of teaching and by the cunning and craftiness of people in their deceitful scheming. Instead, speaking the truth in love, we will grow to become in every respect the mature body of Him who is the head, that is, Christ. From him the whole body, joined and held together by every supporting ligament, grows and builds itself up in love, as each part does its work.

Childish or immature love is the kind that is tossed back and forth by our expectations of others' responses to it. Several years into my marriage, I made a decision about love that changed my life. I decided that I would love my wife in every way possible, whether she responded to it, cared about it, or did the same. I stopped putting conditions on it and looking for what I considered an appropriate reaction. I'm not saying here that my wife is not loving but that my love for her is not based on the degree of her love for me. Loving me is her responsibility. The freedom I experienced from loving her without conditions liberated me from taking on that responsibility, which is impossible anyway. Eventually, it became clear that I needed to extend that kind of love to everyone. There is gratifying liberation in unconditional love, especially for those who discipline themselves to consistently give it.

The leg of love is initially "machined" by our disciplined acceptance and submission to the reality of God's love for us and how He has demonstrated that love through Jesus Christ. It is proven genuine, distinctively shaped, smoothed and beautifully polished by the disciplined way we unconditionally love each other.

THE LEG OF FELLOWSHIP

My wife and I have attended numerous seminars on marriage throughout our married life, sought out counsel when needed, renewed our wedding vows, and had countless conversations about our relationship. We participated in these activities not because our relationship was weak or full of problems but because we wanted the kind of covenantal fellowship with each other that we vowed to pursue. We grew into that relationship, but we had to work at it to get there. The definition of fellowship from chapter 8 was described as, "Our intentional and knowledgeable agreement on what God has done through Christ that we live out with Him and together in harmonious community." When I think of the efforts my wife and I made to deepen the fellowship we have in our marriage, something has become very clear to me that applies to all relationships. Relationships evolve according to the way we shape them. And their shape will be defined in direct proportion to the degree in which truth and love shape us. Godly relationships require being committed to living out truth and love. We can't nurture genuine fellowship in any relationship without them. And it's why the faith disciplines are so relevant and effective in nurturing the kind of meaningful relationships—those of fellowship—that He desires for His church and with Him.

Ephesians 5:21–33[4] uses the metaphor of a marriage relationship to illustrate what this should look like. It provides key ingredients for shaping our relationships in the church:

reverence for Christ
submission to one another
love
giving
taking responsibility for and watching over the relationship
concern for the other's spiritual well-being
nurture and care
Respect

All of these require truth and love. We discipline ourselves to follow the truth of how God teaches us how to behave toward one another. We discipline ourselves to love each other the way Jesus loved us.

The takeaway from chapter 8 was to "Watch over and care for your fellowship with God and His church in the same way that you watch over and care for your life." This involves our discipline in developing godliness in our relationships and guarding their integrity. Two important aspects of this need to be understood.

First, fellowship can be injured or broken. Godly relationships require constant attention and nourishment, just like a garden does. When left uncared for, weeds of apathy can choke the life out of them. The lack of the water of love can cause them to wilt and weaken; inattention to providing the nutrients of the truth stunts their development and causes disease, and the lack of exposure to sunlight—the light of Jesus Christ—separates them from their purpose and fruitfulness. Scriptures emphasize that we watch over our fellowship with God and with each other.

We watch over these relationships with truth and love. Jesus exemplified this when He was tempted by Satan to break His fellowship with His Heavenly Father. He defended this relationship with "It is Written." He loved and valued this relationship more than all the adulation, acceptance, fame, and power this world could offer. And Satan will offer it in subtle ways that appeal to each of us. Often his offer will be made through people who knowingly or unknowingly attempt to distract, divide, dilute, and eventually destroy the godliness of our relationships. The truth and love that God reveals in His Word are the fences that keep the predators out.

> Don't love the world and what it offers. Those who love the world don't have the Father's love in them. Not everything that the world offers, physical gratification, greed, and extravagant lifestyles, comes from the Father. It comes from the world, and the world and its evil desires are passing away. But the person who does what God wants lives forever. (1 John 2:15–17)

We can have only one master and not even a little bit of another. When faced with the thoughts of compromising our fellowship with God, we should respond like Jesus: "Away from me, Satan! For it is written: 'Worship the Lord your God, and serve him only.'" Luke 4:8

We watch over our relationships within God's family with the same discipline and value and allow nothing to injure or break them.

> Make every effort to live in peace with everyone and to be holy; without holiness no one will see the Lord. See to it that no one falls short of the grace

of God and that no bitter root grows up to cause trouble and defile many. (Hebrews 12:14–15)

Be completely humble and gentle; be patient, bearing with one another in love. Make every effort to keep the unity of the Spirit through the bond of peace. There is one body and one Spirit, just as you were called to one hope when you were called; one Lord, one faith, one baptism; one God and Father of all, who is over all and through all and in all. (Ephesians 4:2–6)

But God has put the body together, giving greater honor to the parts that lacked it, so that there should be no division in the body, but that its parts should have equal concern for each other. If one part suffers, every part suffers with it; if one part is honored, every part rejoices with it. Now you are the body of Christ, and each one of you is a part of it. (1 Corinthians 12:24–27)

Second, not all relationships involve fellowship. In fact, God warns us not to have fellowship with certain people, and it is sobering to consider the number of times and emphasis placed on this.

As for a person who stirs up division, after warning him once and then twice, have nothing more to do with him. (Titus 3:10 ESV)

I appeal to you, brothers, to watch out for those who cause divisions and create obstacles contrary to the doctrine that you have been taught; avoid them. (Romans 16:17 ESV)

If anyone comes to you and does not bring this teaching, do not receive him into your house or give him any greeting. (2 John 1:10 ESV)

People will be lovers of themselves, lovers of money, boastful, proud, abusive, disobedient to their parents, ungrateful, unholy, without love, unforgiving, slanderous, without self-control, brutal, not lovers of the good, treacherous, rash, conceited, lovers of pleasure rather than lovers of God, having a form of godliness but denying its power. Have nothing to do with such people. (2 Timothy 3:2–5)

The reason is that relationships affect us in a godly or ungodly way. While godly relationships help us build our faith, there is perhaps no more powerful enticement to draw us away from faith than unholy relationships.

1 Corinthians 15:33:
Do not be deceived: Evil company corrupts good habits (NKJV).
Don't fool yourselves. Bad friends will destroy you (CEV).
Do not be fooled. Bad companions ruin good character (GNT).

Do not try to work together as equals with unbelievers, for it cannot be done. How can right and wrong be partners? How can light and darkness live together? How can Christ and the Devil agree? What does a believer have in common with an unbeliever? (2 Corinthians 6:14–15 GNT)

It is important to understand that while we are not to develop a relationship of fellowship with those who have turned away from God, we are still to love them, just as God does. All fellowship involves love, but all love does not include fellowship. The difference has to do with our allegiance of heart and the covenantal depth of the relationship.

Although we are surrounded by unbelief in this world and are to guard ourselves against fellowship with it, God has given each of us a ministry to reconcile people back to Him through Christ. We all came into our relationship with God and the church because of someone's love for and attention to us. That love, grounded in truth, brought us into fellowship. The primary purpose of our relationship with those outside of Christ's church is that of loving concern for the value of their life and future and helping them see the purposes God has for them in relation to this.

> But dedicate your lives to Christ as Lord. Always be ready to defend your confidence [in God] when anyone asks you to explain it. However, make your defense with gentleness and respect. (1 Peter 3:15 GWT)

The leg of fellowship is initially "machined" by the family relationship we entered when we became followers of Jesus and members of His church. It is distinctively shaped, smoothed, and beautifully polished as we faithfully define, nurture, and protect it with truth and love.

THE PERSONIFICATION OF THE
FAITH DISCIPLINES

Just as Jesus personified truth, love, and fellowship, the faith disciplines defined His life. He didn't simply tell His followers to practice them. They were evident in His life. Even at twelve, He was in the temple discussing the scriptures with the teachers, and "everyone who heard Him was amazed at his understanding and answers." His disciplined and intentional prayer life, times of solitude and silence, honest confessions to His Heavenly Father, encouragement of fasting, and simplicity of His needs are mentioned throughout the New Testament, especially by the Gospel writers. He epitomized the communal disciplines as He publicly submitted Himself to God, worshipped and fellowshipped with His followers, exemplified a servant's heart, mentored His followers, and focused on helping and healing all people.

It is this Jesus that we are to emulate in the practice of the faith disciplines.

> Let us keep our eyes fixed on Jesus, on whom our faith depends from beginning to end. He did not give up because of the cross! On the contrary, because of the joy that was waiting for him, he thought nothing of the disgrace of dying on the cross, and he is now seated at the right side of God's throne. (Hebrews 12:2 GNT)

As Jesus finished His Sermon on the Mount, He concluded by telling us that a godly life requires dedication and discipline to establish a solid foundation. That foundation causes our faith to withstand and flourish no matter the circumstances around us.

> So then, anyone who hears these words of mine and obeys them is like a wise man who built his house on rock. The rain poured down, the rivers flooded over, and the wind blew hard against that house. But it did not fall, because it was built on rock. (Matthew 7:24)

That rock is Jesus Christ, the personification of truth, love, fellowship, and a life disciplined to faith. He is what faith looks like.

The leg of the faith disciplines is initially "machined" according to the patterns of the legs of Truth, Love, and Fellowship. It is distinctively shaped, smoothed, and beautifully polished by the consistent and dedicated ways we practice them.

In 1989, author and educator Steven Covey published a book that swept through the country and eventually the world like a brush fire. It was titled, *The 7 Habits of Highly Effective People* and has sold over thirty million copies. I believe its popularity is largely because most people want to be more effective in achieving what is important to them, and the book offers some helpful solutions to this. It provides a "road map" that guides people to their destination and helps them avoid being sidetracked by activities and attitudes that interfere with their progress.[5]

For those who are on an intentional journey of faith, our destination is a consecrated life of godliness. We want to be effective in our spiritual growth and maturity. The Faith Disciplines provide the spiritual activities that make truth, love, and fellowship tangible.[6] The Faith Disciplines keep us moving in the direction of what really matters to us and keep us from being sidetracked by endless suggestions, temptations, and deceptive enticements.

In the second chapter of Covey's book, "Begin with the End

in Mind," Covey challenges the reader to imagine his or her own funeral and visualize who is there, what they are saying about you, and how you lived your life. If Jesus were at your funeral, what would He say of you? What if He were to say that which was told by a master to whom he had entrusted his servant with his substance while he was away:

> His master said to him, Well done, good and faithful servant. You have been faithful over a little; I will set you over much. Enter into the joy of your master. (Matthew 25:21)

Our Lord has done so much for us and given so much to bring us into an intimate, powerful, and meaningful relationship with Him. The Faith disciplines are that "little" that we are to steward with consistency and tenacity. We should remind ourselves of the key takeaway from this chapter provided in Galatians 6:7: "Do not be deceived: God cannot be mocked. A man reaps what he sows."

CHAPTER 10

THE STRETCHER OF BEING SPIRITUALLY MINDED

Watch your thoughts, they become your words; watch your words, they become your actions; watch your actions, they become your habits; watch your habits, they become your character; watch your character, it becomes your destiny.

—Lao Tzu

Without a disciplined thought life, the four legs of faith that Jesus personified are left to stand alone without any connection to one another, and their meaning and strength are compromised. When this happens, our faith can become out of balance. We can tend to focus on one or two of these aspects of faith and not give the others the attention they need. We understand that the purpose of our journey of faith is to live more and more like Jesus in how He personified godliness. But the first requirement for learning to *live* like Jesus is that we learn to *think* like Jesus. Thoughts precede our actions. The phrase "I acted without thinking" is rarely used in a positive context!

Much has been written on reading, studying, and memorizing the Bible, but little can be found in the practice of training ourselves to conform our thoughts to it in the way God designed us to.[1] I call it the discipline of being spiritually minded.

I define being spiritually minded as intentionally and consistently choosing to think in a way that honors God and aligns our thoughts with His nature, purposes, and godly behavior. In other words, thinking the way that Jesus thought.

The way we think is the first step we take on our faith journey.

Being spiritually minded unifies the interrelationship, interdependency, and relevance of truth, love, fellowship, and the faith disciplines. In our chair metaphor, I compare being spiritually minded to a stretcher connecting the legs (see illustration on page?) because of its similar function. Like the way the stretcher unites the purpose of each leg, enhances their individual strength, and keeps each leg in its intended position, the way we think has the same function with the legs of faith. The four legs of faith are what we are to be spiritually minded about.

THE ONE QUESTION THAT MUST
BE ANSWERED CORRECTLY

Suppose you were to consider some of the most powerful and well-known sermons that have ever been preached. In that case, you might consider "Sinners in the Hands of an Angry God," by Jonathan Edwards in 1741, Martin Luther's 1518 sermon, "Two Kinds of Righteousness," or The Eternal Name," by Charles Spurgeon in 1855. The list could go on with sermons by John Chrysostom, John Knox, John Wesley, and many others, some of whom are preaching today. These sermons have drawn many to Christ and helped them mature in being His followers.

But on one of the most momentous days in history, the day that many refer to as the birthday of the Christian church, apostle Peter delivered a sermon that immediately changed the lives of about three thousand people that heard him. And even though the words were spoken about two thousand years ago, the impact of their power went on to pierce the hearts and change the lives of literally billions of people and continues to do so to this day.[2]

On that day, thousands of Jews from all over the known world were gathered in Jerusalem to celebrate the Feast of Weeks. The controversial events concerning the life of Jesus were a predominant topic of conversation. Less than two months before this, Jesus had been crucified, buried, and raised from the dead. Hundreds of people had seen Him in His resurrected body, including His disciples, who had also watched Him ascend into heaven about a week earlier. During this time, the Holy Spirit was poured out upon His disciples with visible tongues like fire and caused them to speak in the languages of all the people present on this day of what we now call the day of Pentecost. The effect on the crowd was powerful, bewildering, and astonishing. They began to ask what this meant and why it was happening. In the middle of the tumult, apostle Peter stood up. He boldly addressed the crowd, authoritatively stating that this was the fulfillment of prophecies concerning Jesus the Messiah and validating His life, death, burial, and resurrection. He finished His sermon with one of the most convicting and consequential statements that have ever been written: "Therefore let all Israel be assured of this: God has made this Jesus, whom you crucified, both Lord and Messiah."

> When the people heard this, they were cut to the heart and said to Peter and the other apostles, "Brothers, what shall we do?" Peter replied, "Repent and be baptized, every one of you, in the name of Jesus Christ for the forgiveness of your sins. And you will receive the gift of the Holy Spirit. The

> promise is for you and your children and for all
> who are far off—for all whom the Lord our God
> will call." (Acts 2:36–37)

The passionate response to these words by the crowd and Peter's inspired call to action about them convey God's clarion call to all of humankind: What are you going to do about Jesus Christ?

It is the most life-transforming question to be right about and the most consequential one to be wrong about.

It's a question that underlies the most important decisions of your life.

It can potentially change the direction, value, and character of what defines you.

The correct answer opens the gate to the pathway of a Christ-centered life.[3]

Considering the subject of this chapter, it is the starting point for building the stretcher of being genuinely spiritually minded.

WHAT IT MEANS TO REPENT

Peter's answer provides the response that God wills for every man and woman since that pivotal day: "Repent and be baptized, every one of you, in the name of Jesus Christ."

Baptism is considered the entry point into the kingdom of God, the family of God, and the body of Christ. It symbolizes a momentous lifetime turning point where we are unconditionally forgiven of all our sins, change who is Lord in our lives, and become a new person spiritually by the power of the Holy Spirit. It enables us to begin down the faith pathway to a life of consecrated godliness.

However, it is not the *first* thing Peter charged his listeners with on the day of Pentecost. The first thing he implores his audience to do is to *repent*.

Repentance summons us to absolute and unconditional surrender to God as Sovereign. It is most often associated with contrition and being conscience-stricken about sinful behavior in our past. It includes penitence and being disposed to change one's life for the better. But how can one repent of these failures of conscience and behavior without recognizing them? If you don't think you have sinned, how can you, and why would you, confess them as such and ask forgiveness for them?

Those questions are answered when we clearly understand the *initial* focus of repentance. In the New Testament, only one Greek word, translated *repentance* literally means "to change the mind." Repentance begins with a turning or changing of the mind. When you really change your mind about something, it will change the way you talk and act about it. Author Ray Pritchard describes it as: "Repentance initiates a decisive change in direction. It's a change of mind that leads to a shift in thinking, a change of attitude and values, and a change in how you live."[4]

Peter's response to the question of "What shall we do?" was to confront the Jews with the first and most crucial act of repentance: *changing the way they thought about Jesus.* This challenge has been offered to all of humanity ever since. Until we recognize Jesus as both Lord and Messiah, we will never recognize actual sin or spiritual error in our lives. Our attempts at being spiritually minded will have no source of reference or point of origin.

Repentance begins by *turning our thoughts away* from erroneous beliefs about Jesus and *toward* who He truly is. If you want to be a spiritually minded follower of Jesus, this is the starting point.

Jesus as the Lord and Messiah is the anchor that tethers our thoughts to God.

BEING SPIRITUALLY MINDED REQUIRES A LIFESTYLE OF REPENTANT THINKING

Often, repentance seems to be left at the door once we are baptized and enter Christ's church. But repentance doesn't stop at salvation. We are faced with the need to repent, or turn our thoughts from ungodly ones to those that are godly every day—sometimes many times a day. It's a signature habit of godliness that we take with us on our faith journey. It's a key component of being spiritually minded.

Understanding and submitting to the truth of who Jesus is qualifies as our first act of repentance. While our thoughts concerning this are the most important ones we will ever have, they are hardly the last ones! Current research has concluded that the average human has over six thousand thoughts per day, totaling over two million per year.[5] Progress on our faith journey requires that we watch over each of them to align with the way Christ thought. God holds us accountable for thinking like Jesus.

> We tear down arguments and every presumption
> set up against the knowledge of God, and we take
> captive every thought to make it obedient to Christ.
> (2 Corinthians10:5)

Every day we have the responsibility to make six thousand thoughts obedient to Christ! Are you kidding? How is that even possible? Yet, despite how daunting this may seem, God would never command or require us to do something impossible. That would be contrary to His nature.

> He encourages us when He tells us: "For our love
> for God means that we obey his commands. And
> his commands are not too hard for us. (1 John
> 5:3 GNT)

Making our thoughts obedient to Christ is not a burden or unachievable. It's liberating and brings abundant peace and joy to our lives. But it does require effort. It is a vital part of the discipline of training ourselves to be godly.[6] It requires a mind-set of repentant thinking where we consistently turn our thoughts to a godly standard.

The habit of repentant thinking establishes a godly pattern for becoming spiritually minded and allows us to stay on course on our journey of faith.

VALIDATING BEING SPIRITUALLY MINDED

In our Western culture, we tend to think of thoughts and actions as separate entities, where one can function without the other. But in eastern culture, in which the Bible was written, they are considered one and the same. Even the ancient Chinese philosopher Lao Tzu, is quoted as saying:

> Watch your thoughts, they become your words; watch your words, they become your actions; watch your actions, they become your habits; watch your habits, they become your character; watch your character, it becomes your destiny.

He not only tied our thoughts to our words and actions but, ultimately, our destination! In other words, our thoughts are the starting point for our eventual destination. And as we travel on our journey of faith to that promised land of Godly consecration, the way we choose to think will govern our progress. Everything we do started as a thought. Why would we allow ourselves to harbor thoughts that point in a direction opposed to godly behavior? What is the benefit of that? How does that honor and love God? With this in mind, it is helpful to consider our thoughts as part of our behavior.

The way we think, what we allow our minds to focus on, and the thoughts we harbor and value are at the center of personal transformation to being Christlike in our living. If we don't live like a follower of Jesus, it's essentially because we don't think like a follower of Jesus.

Nowhere in scripture are we told that God will take over our thoughts and make us think in a certain way. That's up to us. We are responsible for the thoughts we entertain. Being spiritually minded is a vital discipline that God has much to say about in His word.

First Corinthians provides us with an essential truth about what our minds are capable of.

> Who has known the mind of the Lord so as to instruct him? But we have the mind of Christ. (1 Corinthians 2:16)

We obviously don't have the mind of Christ in a literal way. This is the figure of speech hyperbole, which is used often in scripture to purposely exaggerate to an extreme to make a point. Perhaps you have been told "you have your father's eyes" or "your mother's laugh." You don't literally have your parent's eyes or laugh, but you so closely resemble them that these attributes remind people of your parents because you are like them. The verse is better understood to mean we have a mind "very much like" Christ. And with that likeness come similar capabilities and strengths. If we have a mind very much like Christ's, we can think very much like He did. Do your thoughts resemble those of Jesus?

God has created us in His image. As we have seen, it is His great desire that we know and understand the truth, love unconditionally, and develop an intimate fellowship with Him and His church. Would He not then have made our minds capable of the mental processes necessary to achieve these attributes?

I believe the practice of disciplining our thoughts to conform to the way Jesus thought is the most essential and foundational principle of being a follower of Jesus. We begin to follow Him by changing the way we think *about* Jesus and mature in following Him as we learn to think *like* Jesus.

THE MIND

When scriptures speak of the mind, they refer to that part of the brain that deals with thinking. This would include cognitive functions and skills such as knowledge, attention, memory, attitudes, judgment and evaluation, reasoning, perception, computation, problem solving, decision-making, and the comprehension of language.

Scriptures have much to say about what the mind is capable of:

It can think	It has attitudes
It can be strengthened	It can be deceived
It can learn	It can be lead astray
It can change	It can be corrupted
It can be confused	It can be renewed
It can be ungodly	It can be godly
It can be out of control	It can be controlled
It can hate	It can love
It can remember	It can forget
It can be grieved	It can be at peace
It can be hardened	It can be blinded
It can be corrupted	It can agree and disagree
It can be persuaded	It can doubt
It can believe	It can be shaken
It can be decisive	It can be indecisive
It can be sober	It can be divided
It can generate emotions	It can choose

| It can reason | It can contemplate |
| It can be distracted | It can be focused |

All these mental capabilities, how they are used, and their outcomes will fall under one of two opposing categories of thinking described in scripture:

Godly	Ungodly
Spiritually minded	Carnally minded
Mind of Christ	Worldly
Mind governed by the spirit	Mind of the flesh
Mind on the things of God	Mind on the things of man
God's thoughts	Human thoughts

There is an additional capability of the mind that is not in the list above, yet it is one of the most significant aspects of our thought life: It can sin.

Jesus made the point in Matthew 5 that a man who even looks at a woman with lustful thoughts is committing adultery. If we can commit adultery with our thoughts, what other sins are possible by how we think? Doesn't all sinful behavior begin as a sinful thought?

There is a powerful illustration of this in the Gospel of Mark. The context describes a confrontation between Jesus and Peter concerning Jesus's prophecy of His death and resurrection. In this record, Jesus makes a distinction between the two different ways of thinking. This record also conveys one of the strongest personal rebukes by Jesus recorded in the scriptures.

> But when Jesus turned and looked at His disciples,
> he rebuked Peter. "Get behind me, Satan!" he said.
> "*You do not have in mind* the concerns of God, but

merely human concerns" (Mark 8:33, *emphasis added*).[7]

Jesus is rebuking Peter not just over his words but over how he was *allowing himself to think*! He was criticizing him for not thinking in a godly way. The comedian Flip Wilson's character Geraldine Jones frequently excuses her bad behavior by saying, "The devil made me do it." But Jesus placed the responsibility of how Peter chose to think squarely on Peter. The exact requirement of taking responsibility for how we think has been given to us.

Another important lesson here is that Peter's loyalty or faithfulness to Jesus is not being questioned. Peter was a devout follower and disciple of Jesus—he was passionate, loyal, and had sacrificed and suffered to follow Jesus. Yet despite this, Jesus rebukes him for the way he is thinking.

It makes the point that no matter our love for Jesus, loyalty to him, involvement in ministry, love for Christ's church, or maturity in our faith, we always need to watch over what we allow ourselves to think about and where we allow our minds to go. There is no area of our lives where our thoughts are insignificant or inconsequential.

Peter's words revealed what he was thinking. What do our words reveal about our thoughts? If Jesus were to hear the words that come out of our mouths, would he rebuke us for any of the ways we allow ourselves to think? Are our *thoughts* pleasing to God? We should ask ourselves which of the two minds defined here in Romans 8 defines our thought life:

> Those who live according to the flesh have *their minds set on what the flesh desires*; but those who live in accordance with the Spirit *have their minds set on what the Spirit desires*. The mind governed by the flesh is death, but the mind governed by the Spirit is life and peace. (Romans 8:5–6, emphasis added)

Like Peter and all believers, we choose what we think about and what we set our minds on. No matter where we are in our walk of faith—from the first day we decide to follow Jesus through growing into discipleship—the way we allow ourselves to think is at the core of our Christian life.

IT TAKES LOVE TO BE SPIRITUALLY MINDED

The discipline of being spiritually minded is not only about controlling our thoughts. It's about *why* we control them. It is crucial that in our endeavors to be like Jesus, we must think like Jesus, but it's deeper than just a mental exercise. It's an exercise of humility, submission, and surrender motivated by a genuine love for our Heavenly Father in response to His love for us.[8]

> Don't you realize that it is God's kindness that is
> trying to lead you to him and change the way you
> think and act? (Romans 2:4 GWT)

How can we not respond to God with love when we consider God's lengths to express His love for us? He has brought us into His family and forgiven us of our rebellion against Him and the selfish ways that we have behaved toward others. He sacrificed the life of His own son to bring us into fellowship with Him. He is always there for us, even if we have not been there for Him.

Like the prodigal son that Jesus spoke of in the gospel of Luke, we have often squandered the rich blessings that God has freely given us, yet, when we finally repent and turn back to Him, He not only welcomes us with open arms but celebrates our return.[9] How heartbreaking it must have been for God to watch His son being beaten and tortured when all He had ever done was be a loving, loyal, and obedient son to Him and love people with His father's love. But do you know why He allowed it to happen and didn't stop it?

Because of you and me.

The price that He and His son paid was worth it to them for us to return to Him in fellowship.

When we are tempted to "turn back toward Egypt" and away from Jesus with our thoughts—thoughts of envy, selfishness, lust, greed, fear, anger, unbelief, and idolatry—we should ask ourselves: Did Jesus ever turn away from anyone for those reasons? Did He ever have a love problem? Do we? When those temptations come, and they surely will, our love for God will compel us to turn our thoughts back toward Him.

In summary, without truth, we have no trustworthy thoughts to turn our minds to. Absent the love for God as our purpose behind being spiritually minded, the work of the Spirit of God is eviscerated. Without the engaged fellowship of the Holy Spirit, the discipline of being spiritually minded devolves into a mental exercise akin to the power of positive thinking. Left to our own efforts only, spirituality becomes centered on our abilities to transform ourselves. This may work in losing weight, changing some habits, or increasing our vocabulary, but when it comes to being transformed to be Christlike, we need the supernatural work of the Spirit of God. On the other hand, if we rely only on the work of the Holy Spirit to experience spiritual transformation and make no efforts to align and hold our thoughts captive to the truth, we wind up with an emotional spirituality that is erroneously measured by the positive or negative circumstances of our daily life and whether we are "happy."

It is the work of the Father, the Son, and the Holy Spirit, *as well as us* that brings the transformative power of being spiritually minded into a living reality.

The stretcher of being spiritually minded is initially "machined" by our disciplined efforts to watch over our thoughts and continually align them with the word of God as Jesus personifies it. It is distinctively shaped, smoothed, and beautifully polished as we change the source of the thoughts that define our reality, learn to love God with our minds, and intentionally fellowship with the scriptures.

———————

When we become spiritually minded in the way that Jesus personified, it connects all the aspects of faith together—truth, love, fellowship, and the faith disciplines. It completes the design for the strong, enduring, and transformative faith that God intended. We then have the complete set of directions for our journey of faith and can make measurable progress in them toward a life of consecrated godliness.

As we read and study the scriptures and discipline our thoughts to be captive to its truth, there is a helpful, humbling, and convicting certainty to remember: It's not just words on a page we are setting our minds upon. It is the Lord Himself.

> I have set the Lord always before me. Because He is
> at my right hand, I shall not be moved. (Psalm 16:8)

CHAPTER 11

BUILDING FIVE HABITS FOR BEING SPIRITUALLY MINDED

Habit is the intersection of knowledge (what to do), skill (how to do), and desire (want to do).
—*Stephen R. Covey*

Consider the essential function of your mind when it comes to spirituality: We use our minds to understand the meaning, importance, and relevance of truth, love, fellowship, and the faith disciplines. Without developing this understanding, we have no true north for our faith journey.

We use our minds to discern and provide perspective on how they are interrelated and firmly attached to each other. Without this, we can develop "blind spots" about what is lacking or needful in our faith.

We use our minds to *visualize* what these four legs should look like as we live them out. Without this, we lose sight of our direction and the ability to evaluate our progress.

We use our minds to formulate and commit to the way we will carry out God's plan for maturing in and strengthening our faith.

Without this, we cannot move forward with determination and single-mindedness on our journey toward godliness.

When it comes to being spiritually minded, the model set before us is the mind of Christ. To effectively grow in our practice of thinking like Jesus, we must learn how to use these essential functions of our mind to align our thoughts with the way God designed us to think. God did not design our minds to be put on autopilot when it comes to any aspect of life, including growing in faith. The King James Version of the Bible famously translates Proverbs 23:7: "For as a man (a person) thinketh in his heart, so is he."

We could insert the four legs of faith into this verse to say: for as a man (a person) thinketh in his heart (about truth, about love, about fellowship, and the faith disciplines) so is he.

It is the practice of disciplining our minds to think about how God designed them that connects and unites these components that form the complete structure of our faith. Making up this practice are five essential principles that provide us with the method for *how* we train ourselves to be spiritually minded.

Trust in the power of the Holy Spirit at work in your mind.

Several years ago, I went on a hiking and climbing expedition in a remote national wilderness area of New Mexico with a Christian organization. As part of this experience, I was left by myself for three days on the side of a mountain to fast and pray. All I had was a sleeping bag, some bottles of water, and my Bible. The remoteness and isolation of the experience were unsettling at first. I could look out onto the desert far below me and see no signs of human life for miles. In the solitude and stillness of this place, I was alone with my thoughts. As I spent time reading the scriptures, praying, and talking to God, I experienced an overwhelming sense of the presence and power of the Holy Spirit like never before. It reminded me that God was with me even in a secluded physical location, and I was not alone.

But perhaps the most desolate locations of all are the dark

corners of our thoughts. Those places where ungodliness seems to refuse to leave. But even and especially here, God has promised us that He will never leave us or forsake us.[1] Depending on your background—your upbringing, bad choices, or deeply embedded habits of sin—these corners can be the most intimidating. The challenge of putting off thoughts rooted in our past and putting on ideas of the new self-nature of righteousness can seem difficult, if not impossible. But you are neither alone in this nor left without God's help. God has provided the Holy Spirit to empower us to change how we think.

> The Spirit searches all things, even the deep things of God. For who knows a person's thoughts except their own spirit within them? In the same way no one knows the thoughts of God except the Spirit of God. What we have received is not the spirit of the world, but the Spirit who is from God, so that we may understand what God has freely given us. This is what we speak, not in words taught us by human wisdom but in words taught by the Spirit, explaining spiritual realities with Spirit-taught words. The person without the Spirit does not accept the things that come from the Spirit of God but considers them foolishness, and cannot understand them because they are discerned only through the Spirit. (1 Corinthians 2:11–14)

Without the Spirit of God at work in our lives, we cannot understand the spiritual realities of life in a significant manner. The Spirit of God gives us spiritual eyesight and understanding that illuminates the word of God to us. It provides us with a depth of discernment about the scriptures that is not possible without it. We need not fear or doubt the spiritual capabilities of our minds because Almighty God has given them to us through His Spirit.

> But the Advocate, the Holy Spirit, whom the father will send in my name, will teach you all things and will remind you of everything I have said to you. (John 14:26)

It is important to note that the Holy Spirit will *remind* us of what Jesus said. If we are going to be *reminded*, that means it had to have been in our minds in the first place! The discipline of being spiritually minded requires a partnership with God. The verse also says that the Spirit reminds us of what *Jesus* said. The Holy Spirit does not bring thoughts to mind that contradict the truth that He taught! That's how we know that the in-working of the spirit of God is genuine.

> The weapons we fight with are not the weapons of the world. On the contrary, they have divine power to demolish strongholds. (2 Corinthians 5:9)

No matter the strongholds that your past may have upon you, they can be demolished by the spirit of power, love, and sound judgment that God has given you.[2] These are now your God-given and God-powered abilities. But you must use them. God cannot think for you. Each of us must fight for the truth to prevail in our minds for these truths to become a visible reality in our lives.

> Do not conform to the pattern of this world, but be transformed by the renewing of your mind. Then you will be able to test and approve what God's will is—his good, pleasing and perfect will. (Romans 12:2)

Scripture says that transformation is connected to the source of the thoughts we conform our minds to. God will not *make us* think a certain way, but He has *made us be able* to think a certain way. Empowered by the Holy Spirit *and* our disciplining our minds to believe the truth of who we are in Christ, we are transformed into a new creation.

LEARN TO LOVE GOD WITH YOUR MIND

A perceptive preacher once asked, "What does love require of me?" Our response to that question usually revolves around our words and behavior. But we need to go a little deeper. We need to understand what precedes our words and behavior and ask, "What does love require about the way I think?"

There is a correlation between how much we value and love God and how much we think about Him and allow His word to govern our thoughts. We usually think about what we love and what is most important and precious to us. We should ask ourselves what the predominant subject we think about most of the time is. What is competing for most of our thoughts? What do your thoughts tell you about what you love and value?

This singular purpose of being spiritually minded is clarified by an important truth that we must imbed deeply into our hearts: intentionally and consistently bringing our thoughts to align with Christ's is, at its core, an act of loving God.

When you consider that our thoughts determine our behavior, we must first think with love to behave with love. This was made clear when Jesus taught us that we are to love God with our minds.

> One of the teachers of the law came and heard them
> debating. Noticing that Jesus had given them a good
> answer, he asked Him, Of all the commandments,

which is the most important? The most important
one, answered Jesus, is this: "Hear, O Israel: The
Lord our God, the Lord is one. Love the Lord your
God with all your heart and with all your soul and
with *all your mind* and with all your strength."
(Mark 12:28–30, emphasis added)

The word translated *mind* here literally means thinking
something through, the activity of thinking, or the faculty of
thought. We often talk of loving God with our heart, soul, and
strength, but not so much about loving God with all our minds
(thoughts). Yet, Jesus said that we are to love God with *all* our minds.
In effect, He says *all of what our mind is capable of.* If Jesus said we
can love God with all our mental capabilities, it must not only be
necessary, it must also be possible!

We love God with our minds by choosing to fill our minds with
His thoughts or words. We demonstrate this love by the way we
value, entertain, consider, submit to, contemplate, and give honor to
their truth. Perhaps the most important consequence of *thinking* in
ways contrary to God's word is that we are unloving toward Him,
turning away from the most important commandment.

How much time do you spend filling your mind with the word
of God in study, memorization, and meditation, compared to, say,
filling your mind with what is in the newspaper, watching television,
or surfing the web? What is the topic of most of your conversations?
Do these activities draw you into or away from loving God with
your mind? Like Joshua charged Israel to decide whom they serve,
ask yourself whom you serve with your thoughts. The answers to
these questions will give you an indication of who and what you love.

Decide that God's word is the source of the thoughts that define
who you are.

Your self-image influences every aspect of your life. It either limits
or expands what you aspire to in life. It affects every relationship you

have. It shapes your confidence in your abilities and interests. Most importantly, it reflects how you interact with God.

The most challenging contest that Christians engage in is won or lost between our ears. It's a competition over whether our thoughts reflect truth or falsehoods, unconditional love or quid pro quo, godly fellowship or superficial relationships. Usually, the foes we compete with are the thoughts that identify us with the person we used to be before we decided to follow Jesus. God challenges us to choose His word to be the source for the thoughts that form our self-image and to act on those words.

> To put off your old self, which belongs to your former manner of life and is corrupt through deceitful desires, and to be renewed in the spirit of your minds, and to put on the new self, created after the likeness of God in true righteousness and holiness. (Ephesians 4:22–24)

Who we are in Christ is not something we earned or can take credit for. We need not be concerned about being good enough to deserve it. We're not! It is a gift to us through God's unconditional love. Loving God includes accepting this gift and making it our reality.

Whatever our past, we begin to distance ourselves from it as we change the source of the thoughts we entertain. The source of our reality now becomes the truth given to us by the Creator of reality. The further we journey down our path of faith, the further our past becomes behind us, and finally, we get so far away from it that it no longer influences us. Eventually, we can't even see it anymore.[3]

What is essential to be aware of are the thoughts we *entertain*. Entertaining thoughts is not the same as the random thoughts that blow through our minds for a second or two. To entertain a thought is to hold onto it. It's a thought you allow to sit down, make itself comfortable, and have a conversation with. If we entertain them long enough, eventually, they move in and live with us. They become defining characteristics of our self-identity.

> "It's not what you say out of your mouth that determines your life, it's what you whisper to yourself that has the most power!"[4]

We whisper to ourselves the thoughts that we allow to define our reality. Sometimes the whisper is so soft that we don't consciously hear it if we're not paying attention but subtly accept it. Sometimes, they have been whispered so frequently that we don't really pay attention to their source anymore or question if they are true. Often, they are thoughts from long ago, perhaps from our childhood, teen years, or as young adults. Yet even over time, those whispers can seem as powerful as a scream. Those are the words that unassumingly speak to our hearts about how we frame our opinions, attitudes, and decisions. They affect how we treat our spouses, children, coworkers, neighbors, and other Christians. They determine the standards for our work ethic, worldview, ethics, and morals. Most importantly, when we look in the mirror, they are what we perceive to be the reality that defines the identity of the person we see.

> You have searched me, Lord, and you know me. You know when I sit and when I rise; you perceive my thoughts from afar. You discern my going out and my lying down; you are familiar with all my ways. Before a word is on my tongue you, Lord, know it completely. (Psalm 139:1–4)

Our God understands who we are more than we do of ourselves. He should be the source of the way we think of ourselves. What are the words you allow to define who you are?

DEVELOP A RELATIONSHIP OF
FELLOWSHIP WITH THE SCRIPTURES

When I first became of follower of Jesus, I became consumed with memorizing scripture. I wrote down the most important categories of my life that I wanted to change and then listed scriptures that I thought gave me the perspective I needed. The categories were overcoming fear, being prosperous, hoping for the future, receiving healing, and having spiritual strength. Over time, I memorized hundreds of scriptures relative to these categories and carried around a list of them that I would refer to throughout the day.

This habit gave me a great deal of truth about these areas of life that I needed to have, but I didn't see the results I wanted despite this. The words often seemed powerless when confronted with believing and trusting them when I was in the situations I was trying to overcome or change. I remember one verse that I used to hang my hat on was Philippians 4:13: "I can do all this through him who gives me strength." I must have recited this verse to myself thousands of times, but the "all things" turned out to be "very few things," and I wasn't experiencing the power of God in my life to any measurable degree. Why was this? Why wasn't the truth setting me free like Jesus promised?

Surprisingly, the answer I needed was initially shaped in the form of a cold remedy television commercial in the early 1980s. In it, a father with a persistent cough was approached by his little son, dressed in a doctor's outfit, who had two large cookies in his outstretched hands. He then sternly told his father, "Take two of these and call me in the morning!" The line was initiated by doctors prescribing aspirin as an overnight solution for pain. I enjoyed that commercial and thought about it occasionally. But at some point, I believe God used it to open my eyes to see that this was precisely what I was doing with His word! In mass doses, I was using the scriptures like some sort of magic pill or overnight fix for my spiritual ills. They had become more of a quasi-spiritual set of positive affirmations rather than God lovingly speaking to me through them. I had, in effect, developed the cavalier attitude toward God of "take two scriptures and call me in the morning!"

Like I did, you may value the Bible for its truth, be encouraged by its loving words, comforted by its promises, and self-assured by the hope it conveys. You can be consummately disciplined and dedicated to knowing it, even memorizing much of it. But you can still fail to benefit from its transformative power if read and understood with some blind spots concerning why God has given it to you. There can be a blind spot in our relationship with the scriptures that emasculates their faith-building and spiritual impact on us. Without being *surrendered to the source* of those words and genuinely loving them because of the God they reveal, they can become:

a series of dos and don'ts
a checklist for maintaining our self-righteousness
relying on them only in "emergency situations"
a series of affirmations for positive thinking like those in a self-help book

God's word is alive and powerful! It is meant to draw us into an intimate and transformative relationship with Him by revealing Him to us. I believe that God desires that we have this kind of relationship with His word—a relationship defined by what He has done for us through Christ. He wants our relationship with the scriptures to be one of fellowship. His word is that real and personal.[5]

This fellowship with God's word is recognizable and real when:

We approach the scriptures with a loving attitude of surrender to conform our lives to what they say because of our love for our Heavenly Father.

We study them with an attitude that they are holy and infallible because God is their source.

We learn and live them because we desire to be holy, godly, and consecrated to the faith that God has called us to.

We recognize and respect that they are God speaking to us personally.

The blessings of knowing scripture come not from the amount of it that we know but from how much we delight in and have fellowship with what we know. Gospel writer John described remaining in Christ by remaining in His words. We are not only to hold His words but be held by them!

> If you remain in me and my words remain in you,
> ask whatever you wish, and it will be done for you.
> This is to my father's glory, that you bear much fruit,
> showing yourselves to be my disciples. (John 15:7–8)

To remain means to join, abide, or live in, dwell, or stay in. The Message Bible beautifully describes it to mean: "Make yourselves at home with me and my words at home in you."

Being at home usually recalls safety and security, peace and comfort, rest, and a sense of permanence. When someone inquires where you live, a picture of your home comes to mind. If asked, you can describe in detail—each room, how it's decorated, and what is inside it, because you live there, and you're familiar with it.

Jesus desires that our minds are a home for Him. And the longer He lives there by way of our thoughts, the more familiar we become with the details of a life lived in Christ. When He makes His home in our thoughts, we have a sense of spiritual safety, security, peace, comfort, and rest. Like our physical homes, we can arrange and decorate our minds with the beauty of the truth. When our thoughts remain in fellowship with the word of our Lord, we remain in fellowship with Him.

MAKE A COVENANT WITH YOUR MIND

When the book *Every Man's Struggle*[6] came out about twenty years ago, I was drawn to a section about Job. Job was a man described as one who worshiped God and was faithful to him. He was a good man, careful not to do anything evil.[7] To stay faithful to God concerning sexual lust, Job did something unique and never mentioned anywhere else in the Bible.

> I made a covenant with my eyes not to look lustfully
> at a young woman. (Job 31:1)

This may sound odd and impossible, but Job was a regular person, just like you and me, yet he successfully kept his covenant and was blessed for it. And it illustrates a level of loving obedience to God that we can commit to with our thoughts.

Make a covenant with our minds like Job did with his eyes:

A covenant not to allow our minds to entertain thoughts that are outside of the obedience of Christ

A covenant to reject thoughts contrary to what the scripture says about every area of life

A covenant to be faithful to repentant thinking

A covenant to keep Paul's exhortation to the believers in Philippi:

> Finally, brothers and sisters, whatever is true,
> whatever is noble, whatever is right, whatever is
> pure, whatever is lovely, whatever is admirable—if
> anything is excellent or praiseworthy—think about
> such things. (Philippians 4:8)

If a covenant can be made to discipline ourselves to control everything we look at, it can be made to control the thoughts we entertain.

Have you ever felt like you have two minds? Like your mind is living a double life? Like the proverbial little devil speaking into one ear and the little angel speaking into the other, are there two voices with which you are conversing? God sets a choice before us:

> Submit yourselves, then, to God. Resist the devil,
> and he will flee from you. Come near to God and
> he will come near to you. Wash your hands, you
> sinners, and purify your hearts, you double-minded.
> (James 4:7–8)

We submit to God by submitting to His word.[8] Without this, we are left powerless and even clueless in recognizing Satan's endless stream of suggestions. Our primary line of defense in resisting Satan is with our thoughts. If Satan can win in our thinking, he will eventually win in our hearts. His most potent weapon is that of deception, but it is powerless when confronted by the truth of God believed. When Satan realizes that we don't listen to him, he moves on.

Our hearts become purified as our thoughts are purified. Something that is pure is free of contamination.

> And the words of the Lord are flawless, like silver
> purified in a crucible, like gold refined seven times.
> (Psalm 12:6)

God's word is pure. No other words match their integrity. We can make a covenant with our minds to set our thoughts on His word and purify our minds.

> Therefore, since you have been raised with Christ,
> strive for the things above, where Christ is seated
> at the right hand of God. Set your minds on things

above, not on earthly things. For you died, and your life is now hidden with Christ in God. When Christ, who is your life, appears, then you also will appear with Him in glory. (Colossians 3:1–4)

And we set our minds upon the truth because they are spiritual words that involve and call upon the Holy Spirit's help to understand and live them out.

We are faced with the trial of being spiritually minded with every thought. As we persevere in it, we mature into Christlike thinking. Is it a thought that meets the test of Philippians 4:8: whatever is true, whatever is honorable, whatever is just, whatever is pure, whatever is lovely, and whatever is commendable? Is it a thought that Jesus would entertain?

We have considered what is involved in building five habits for becoming spiritually minded:

Trust in the power of the Holy Spirit at work in your mind.
Learn to love God with your mind.
Decide that God's word is the source of the thoughts that define who you are.
Develop a relationship of fellowship with the scriptures.
Make a covenant with your mind.

You'll notice that each one of these habits begins with a verb— an action word. Without acting on building these habits, they will never benefit you. Persevering in them will draw you closer to God, and He will draw closer to you.

———————

At the close of the last chapter, the point was made: "It's not just words on a page we are setting our minds upon, it is the Lord himself." Considering that, as we practice and become proficient in these habits, we accomplish something that is genuinely transforming:

If you remain in me and my words remain in you, ask whatever you wish, and it will be done for you. This is to my father's glory, that you bear much fruit, showing yourselves to be my disciples. (John 15:7–8)

— PART 3 —

LIVING YOUR FAITH

INTRODUCTION

The purpose of understanding faith and shaping its components is that we might live in the way Jesus exemplified. It's time to take what we know and put it into practice as a lifestyle! Faith is not genuine unless it is lived. We are called to be transformed into the men and women that God has called us to be. God redirects us from a life disconnected from Him to one inseparably consecrated to Him in faith:

A life of purpose in sanctified fellowship with Him
A life of spiritual fruitfulness
A life that reflects Jesus Christ
A life that is rich with the blessings of God that can only come when built on a foundation of godly faith
A life of dwelling in the promised land of Godliness

This transformation is described in the epistle to the Ephesians when Paul compares their life before following Jesus with the new life ahead of them on their faith journey.

> That, however, is not the way of life you learned when you heard about Christ and were taught in him in accordance with the truth that is in Jesus. You were taught, about your former way of life, to put off your old self, which is being corrupted by

its deceitful desires; to be made new in the attitude
of your minds; and to put on the new self, created
to be like God in true righteousness and holiness.
(Ephesians 4:20–24)

These final chapters—"Assembling Faith," "Sharing Faith,"
and "The Hope Set Before Us"—provide a picture of a living
faith's life—a life "created to be like God in true righteousness and
holiness."

CHAPTER 12

ASSEMBLING FAITH

A life of reaction is a life of slavery, intellectually and spiritually. One must fight for a life of action, not reaction.

—*Rita Mae Brown*

If you have ever tried to assemble something, you understand the challenges before you. First, you must have a general idea of what you're putting together is supposed to look like. Then you need the proper tools along with accurate instructions. The parts need to be accurately made to fit together correctly. You may make some mistakes and have to do some things over. Sometimes you need some help, and you always need some time.

Perhaps you have never thought of faith as something that needs to be assembled, but there are some significant parallels here. Throughout this study, we have focused on five components of faith that are the primary elements of what faith is composed of. We have used the scriptures as our guidelines for what materials go into making them and how each of these components is individually fashioned. This was summed up in chapters 8 and 9:

The leg of truth is initially "machined" by our persistent,

disciplined, and intentional study of God's Word. It is more deeply, intimately, distinctively shaped, smoothed, and beautifully polished by the other disciplines.

The leg of love is initially "machined" by our humble acceptance and submission to the reality of God's love for us and how He has demonstrated that love through Jesus Christ. It is proven genuine, distinctively shaped, smoothed, and beautifully polished by the disciplined way we unconditionally love each other.

The leg of fellowship is initially "machined" by the family relationship we entered when we became followers of Jesus and members of His church. It is distinctively shaped, smoothed, and beautifully polished as we faithfully define, nurture, and protect it with truth and love.

The leg of the faith disciplines is initially "machined" according to the same patterns as the legs of Truth, Love, and Fellowship. It is distinctively shaped, smoothed, and beautifully polished by the disciplined way we practice them.

The Stretcher of Being Spiritually Minded is initially "machined" by our disciplined efforts to watch over our thoughts and continually align them with the word of God as Jesus personifies it. It is distinctively shaped, smoothed, and beautifully polished as we change the source of the thoughts that define our reality, practice loving God with our minds, and intentionally develop fellowship with the scriptures.

Now we have these five beautiful and godly components of faith. We have identified what they are made of and look like. Each has integrity and value. But if left unassembled, they are just parts that lay on a workbench. God intended for them to have a *combined* function and purpose. Faith is not faith without all these components working together. They need to be correctly assembled for this to happen.

And when something is correctly assembled, it is ready to use.

In this chapter, I would like to offer some practical truth from scripture that gives us the tools and materials we need to assemble these five components to reflect the faith of Jesus Christ—and live them! They consist of three primary requirements:

TAKE OWNERSHIP OF YOUR FAITH

We can be quite possessive when it comes to our stuff. Even when we were little children, we had a sense of what was "ours." We have probably gotten into more than a few fights with our siblings over using our things without permission. We own certain things; they are ours and ours alone, and the more valuable they are to us, the more possessive we are about them. We claim our ownership by describing them as *my* car, house, education, job, family, and even *my* life! And because they belong to us, we take care of them.

In the same way that we are passionate, responsible, and accountable for what we possess, assembling our faith requires that same sense and responsibility of ownership. *Your* faith is precisely that—it belongs to *you* and no one else! And you are responsible for it twenty-four hours every day. No one else will build it for you or give it to you, not even God.[1] He has provided the raw materials, the "lumber," if you will, but you are responsible for shaping it into a base of faith. He has given us the master teacher in Jesus to guide us and provides the enablement through the Holy Spirit.

REVISITING TO A KEY TRUTH IN PETER'S EPISTLE

> His divine power has given us everything we need for life and Godliness through the knowledge of Him who called us by His own glory and excellence. Through these He has given us His precious and magnificent promises, so that through them you may become partakers of the divine nature, now

that you have escaped the corruption in the world
caused by evil desires. (2 Peter 1:3–4)

We must take ownership of God's promises. One of the ways we
do this is to read them like God is speaking to us, like we are the
only person in the room. The scriptures are God speaking to us
individually and personally.

Philippians further encourages us that while God is at work in
us to will and act to fulfill His good purpose, an effort on our part
is required.

> Be energetic in your life of salvation, reverent and
> sensitive before God. That energy is *God's* energy,
> an energy deep within you, God himself willing and
> working at what will give him the most pleasure.[2]
> (Philippians 2:12–13 MESSAGE)

Being reverent and sensitive before God means having an
attitude of sobering accountability because of the weightiness of
our responsibility. In other words, we are to take it very seriously.
We are to own it.

A brief survey of scriptures in the New Testament shows over
sixty references to the term "your faith," depending on the version.
If it's yours, it belongs to you. In one of the most potent revelations
about faith that God has conveyed to us, He reminds us of the value
of genuine faith, a faith that is ours.

> Though you have not seen him, you love him; and
> even though you do not see him now, you believe in
> him and are filled with an inexpressible and glorious
> joy, for you are receiving the end result of your faith,
> the salvation of your souls. (1 Peter 1:8–9)

It is "your faith," the faith that you own, that provides the salvation, or wholeness, of your soul, or as the Aramaic Bible in Plain English puts it, "the life of your soul."

> Each one should test their own actions. Then they can take pride in themselves alone, without comparing themselves to someone else, for each one should carry their own load. (Galatians 6:4–5)

Carrying your load is owning your faith. In other words, assembling your faith can only be done by you. It's a hands-on project, and you'll have to get them dirty with involvement. But there is no more rewarding, satisfying, and transformative activity than faithfully and correctly assembling these faith components.

USE THE RIGHT ADHESIVE

Included in owning the assembly of our faith is the responsibility for using the suitable materials to hold all its components together.

Most times, chairs are brought into my studio for restoration because their joints have become loose. The primary cause of this is the deterioration of the glue that holds them together. When this happens, their strength and purpose are compromised. When it comes to holding the components of faith together, God has given us a "superglue" with the strongest bond possible. It's called love. The love of God is the glue for faith that never fails. It can't be compromised and never wears out. In chapter 6, we read in Galatians 6 that love activates faith. It also binds it together.

> Therefore, as God's chosen people, holy and dearly loved, clothe yourselves with compassion, kindness, humility, gentleness, and patience. Bear with each other and forgive one another if any of you has

a grievance against someone. Forgive as the Lord
forgave you. And over all these virtues put on love,
which binds them all together in perfect unity.
(Colossians 3:12–14)

The problem with using the love of God as the adhesive is that
it is costly. It's going to cost you everything. It will cost you, well,
you! It will cost you your pride, your longing for acceptance by this
world, and the self-centered attitudes that have shaped you. It will
cost you the false ideas and worldly values our culture holds dear
because genuine love never compromises the truth. It cherishes and
obeys what God has to say above everything else. It will cost you the
satisfaction of saying whatever you want and how you want to say
it because it requires speaking the truth and speaking it in love. It
involves the kind of selflessness that values fellowship and unity in
relationships above all else. It compels you to love and forgive people
that are difficult to love, may have hurt you deeply, or are different
from you in ways you don't respect or understand.

Perhaps the highest cost will be abandoning the reason you
believe you are here, and instead, viewing your life from a perspective
that requires you to change your self-identity.

Despite its cost, the love of God is the only thing that has the
necessary strength and longevity to hold our faith together. Our
faith depends on it. Our faith is worth it. Corinthians illustrates just
how powerful the love of God is.

Love is patient, love is kind. It does not envy, it
does not boast, it is not proud. It does not dishonor
others, it is not self-seeking, it is not easily angered,
it keeps no record of wrongs. Love does not delight
in evil but rejoices with the truth. It always protects,
always trusts, always hopes, always perseveres. *Love
never fails.* (1 Corinthians 13:4–8, emphasis added)

Other versions translate the last part of verse 8 as:

Love never fades away.

Love will last forever.

Love never comes to an end.

Love is eternal.

Love never dies.

In other words, love overcomes. Why? Because love is stronger than evil.[3] These words speak to love's strength, dependability, and endurance. There are much cheaper and easier-to-use products out there, but like the common adage says, "You get what you pay for," and Satan has them on sale every day.

Living in the love of God comes with a price. But something we should always keep in mind is that, as costly as it is to us, it relatively inexpensive when you consider what it cost Him.

God recognizes and honors the price we pay and the sacrifices we make for love to bind our faith together.

> The master was full of praise. Well done, my good and faithful servant. You have been faithful in handling this small amount, so now I will give you many more responsibilities. Let's celebrate together! (Matthew 25:21)

Other versions translate the last part of this verse, "Come and share in my happiness," "Share your master's joy," and "Enter into the joy of your lord." When we are faithful to love, it deepens our relationship with God to the point of mutual joy with Him. Could we ever overpay for this?

God *loves* that we are working to assemble a life of faith! Use the love of God as the adhesive that holds the components of your faith together. Love the truth and desire to learn more about it. Love being able to love. Love your fellowship with God and people. Love disciplining your life in obedience to God. And love thinking about faith and how you live it out. Be generous in how you apply the adhesive of love. It's never wasted.

PUT YOUR ASSEMBLY OF FAITH IN THE PROPER PERSPECTIVE

The first time I built a chair was quite an experience. It was not of my design. I was copying another well-made antique chair. I made accurate patterns, reproduced all the parts precisely, and glued and clamped them together with care. But something I failed to do during the process was to stand back and observe it from its overall perspective. I spent all my efforts focused on each part without viewing it as a whole. When I finally did, I was disappointed to see that the entire chair decidedly slanted to the right! I had my teacher critique my work. While he was pleased with much of the work I had done, he reminded me that from time to time, I needed to view my work from different angles to make sure it was balanced and unified as a whole. Even though I made each part accurately, the materials were correct, and the joints were sound, it didn't reflect the design and intent of the original maker, and its stability would be short-lived. So, I had to take it all apart and reassemble it accurately.

As we assemble faith, one of the most essential requirements to remember is that faith is of God's design, not ours. It should look the way that reflects His design. This takes perspective. So how do we do this?

First, we stand back and let our master evaluate our faith with us.

We humbly bring our lives before Him in solitude and prayer. We align and surrender our will to His will. We ask Him through the power of the Holy Spirit to give us the spiritual eyes to see just how genuine our faith is and where we need to change.

The Spirit searches all things, even the deep things of God. For who knows a person's thoughts except their own spirit within them? In the same way no one knows the thoughts of God except the Spirit of God. What we have received is not the spirit of the world, but the Spirit who is from God, so that we may understand what God has freely given us. (1 Corinthians 2:10–12)

As our loving Heavenly Father, God provides us with His Spirit that gives us a perspective of our faith that we cannot acquire or perceive on our own. *Faith is a profoundly spiritual matter*, and we need the Father, the Son, and the Holy Spirit to place and keep it in its genuine perspective.

God loves that we are working at growing in our faith, and He wants us to get it right even more than we do. Our Lord wants our faith to be genuine, and we cannot achieve this without Him.

Second, we stand back with a trusted brother or sister in Christ to evaluate our faith with us.

Now you are the body of Christ, and each one of you is a part of it. (1 Corinthians 12:27)

We need each other! Have you ever considered why? Often, we think of receiving encouragement, getting help when we are in need, enjoying friendships, and overcoming our failings. These are all important, but especially so in growing in faith. I believe one of the most important purposes in our relationships is to help one another put our faith in the godly perspective that makes it complete. We need each other for faith.[4]

God has called us to individual faith and a communal one. What more loving, meaningful, and necessary gift can we provide each other with than helping one another strengthen our godly faith?

> But God has put the body together, giving greater honor to the parts that lacked it, so that there should be no division in the body, but that its parts should have equal concern for each other. If one part suffers, every part suffers with it; if one part is honored, every part rejoices with it. (1 Corinthians 12:24–26)

God has created His church not only for Him but for each other. We are all affected by one another's behavior. And the "equal concern" He speaks of here includes helping each other grow spiritually. We should treasure and respect the importance of being able to speak into each other's lives with doctrine, reproof, and correction about putting our faith in its proper perspective. Often, others can see things about our lives that we are unaware of or need help with.

> As a prisoner for the Lord, then, I urge you to live a life worthy of the calling you have received. Be completely humble and gentle; be patient, bearing with one another in love. Make every effort to keep the unity of the Spirit through the bond of peace. There is one body and one Spirit, just as you were called to one hope when you were called; one Lord, one faith, one baptism; one God and Father of all, who is over all and through all and in all. (Ephesians 4:1–6)

Living the life worthy of what God calls us to is not just an individual one but a call to His entire church. Our efforts to keep the unity of the Spirit include a unified faith. And we need each other to watch over our faith and help us see areas of our lives that compromise it.

My friends, if someone is caught in any kind of
wrongdoing, those of you who are spiritual should
set him right; but you must do it in a gentle way.
And keep an eye on yourselves, so that you will not
be tempted, too. Help carry one another's burdens,
and in this way you will obey the law of Christ
(Galatians 6:1–2 and 9–10 GNT)

The most difficult burdens are those that hinder our faith. What
more significant, more loving service can we provide to one another
but to help remove those weights and obstacles to gain a clearer
perspective of our faith?

Taking ownership of assembling our faith with the love of God
and keeping it in a godly perspective is what forms truth, love,
fellowship, and the faith disciplines into the structure of faith that
God intended. We need to be vigilant in watching over it every day.
It is a key effort we make on our lifetime journey of building the
faith of Jesus Christ.

And in assembling our faith, there is an important takeaway
that God has given us: While you are responsible for constructing
your faith, you are not alone. To ensure your faith is genuine, you
have the Father, the Son, the Holy Spirit, and your brothers and
sisters in Christ.

CHAPTER 13

SHARING FAITH

Our faith becomes stronger as we express it; a growing faith is a sharing faith.

—*Billy Graham*

The first church I was involved with in a significant way was extremely focused on reaching out to people with the good news of Jesus Christ. His commission to make disciples everywhere was considered a priority.[1] We were encouraged and taught how to build speaking about the things of God into our everyday conversations with friends, neighbors, coworkers, and any others we might interact with during our day. Sharing our faith with others became an exciting part of how we lived.

Jan was a friend of mine in this church who was very passionate about what Christ made available to people, but she was frustrated over the lack of opportunity she had to share these things during the week. She worked for the National Park Service, maintaining hiking trails, and spent most of her workdays isolated in the park. It was common for her to spend the entire workweek without seeing a soul.

One evening, she shared her discouragement with our home fellowship group and asked for prayers about it. A few days later, she was clearing some tree limbs from the intersection of a secondary path off the Appalachian Trail. Thomas, a young man spending a couple of months hiking the trail, came along, and Jan struck up a conversation with him. During their exchange, Jan found that Thomas was indeed searching for truth.

She invited him to our small group fellowship, which he attended that evening. Our group was getting ready to start a class about Christian foundational truths, and we invited him to attend. One of the families had a spare bedroom and offered to put him up for the two weeks of the class, and he decided to stay. He was genuinely moved by the Word of God taught, the love showed him, and some answers and hope he was given.

Once the class was over, Thomas got back on the Appalachian Trail and continued his hike. We stayed in touch by mail (there was no internet then) and got him connected with a local church when he returned home. A few years later, he and his wife returned to visit us. He had stayed engaged in his Christian faith and was becoming a well-grounded and faithful disciple.

As much as Thomas, his wife, and our church were thankful for the events surrounding his coming to Christ, my friend Jan was overjoyed. Not only for Thomas's life but for the way God had answered her longing to make a difference with her life in this way. Like the quote by Billy Graham at the beginning of this chapter, sharing her faith with someone else caused hers to become stronger. And this story speaks to a few points I want to make about sharing our faith.

A HOLE IN THE HEART

We need God. No matter our circumstances, until we have a meaningful relationship with Him, there will be a hole in our hearts. It can be a hole of ambiguity about the presence of God, the meaning and consequences of appropriate morality, ethics, or what is truly right or wrong. Sometimes it's a hole of uncertainty about the future in this life and beyond. Often, it's a hole of the fear of rejection, being unaccepted, and failure, for which this world's answers only provide a veneer of assurance. Sometimes people are searching for something and often don't even know what it is. No matter the description of the hole, it's there, because without God, we are all incomplete.

In our American culture, it's rare for someone to have never heard of Jesus, but it's very common for people to be ambivalent about why they need Him. The questions of who He is, why He came, and what their relationship with Him should be, have often been poorly explained, considered unimportant, or even been rejected.

Every life has a story, and the status of one's spiritual life is part of it. Some have understood the need for a relationship with God from an early age because they have been raised and encouraged to recognize and pursue it with intentionality. But for many of us, the pursuit of godliness was absent or minimal in our upbringing. For many, life seems so good, or good enough, that they may not perceive their need for God in their life. A high value is placed on wealth, success, intelligence, social standing, family name, or worldly position. Because of having this world's goods, it might be harder to see that hole, but it's there. Jesus cautioned us with this deception in the Gospel of Luke: "What good is it for someone to gain the whole world, and yet lose or forfeit their very self?" (Luke 9:25).

For others, during or after a tragedy, severe illness, or insurmountable problem they are facing, the hole becomes apparent because of their hopeless circumstances. These situations tend to put our human helplessness and need for God right before us. But there is comfort through the presence of our Lord God through all calamity and misfortune.

> The Lord is near to the brokenhearted and saves the
> crushed in spirit. (Psalm 34:18 ESV)

Sometimes people who had been followers of Jesus have forsaken their journey of faith or turned their back on God *because* of pain and suffering. Anger and bitterness over a personal loss can be powerful triggers to pursue consolation and justice outside of their faith. Yet, the hole remains.

Tragically, many former followers of Christ have walked away from their faith because of their experiences of mistreatment, abuse, or bad theology within the church itself. If this is part of your story, I would ask you to remember that Christ is the head of the church, and we follow Him. He will never abuse or hurt you. Don't give up on Him! He will never give up on you!

People come to Christ for various reasons and from different circumstances, and no one needs Jesus more or less than someone else. Without Christ, there is a hole in someone's heart. Whatever people's story, the bottom line is that they seek God when they realize that only He can fill that hole.

God has given each of us the responsibility to be there for others with answers of truth and love. A humble awareness of this gave my friend a passion for bringing Jesus into someone else's story. And it was the same love and concern that someone else had for you and me that brought us to Christ.

Every life is valuable to God, and because of that, it should be to us.

A HOLE IN THE HEAD

I think sometimes we Christians have a hole in the head about evangelism. I believe Christians spend far too much energy worrying about their ability and effectiveness in communicating the good news of Jesus Christ. We must use some of the common sense that God has given us and trust in the power of our message! I don't remember reading about Bible classes on witnessing, evangelism, or shepherding people in the first century! *How to Win Friends and Influence People*[2] was long from being written. Yet, despite this seeming lack of training, simple fishermen became effective fishers of men.

Today much *has* been written on outreach for churches and strategies for personal evangelism. There *are* all kinds of classes and seminars available to help you become a better communicator. While these resources can be helpful, I believe that we must get into our heads and hearts some self-evident things. And without them, the effectiveness of the resources mentioned will be eviscerated. The "formula" is straightforward: "Consequently, faith comes from hearing the message, and the message is heard through the word about Christ" (Romans 10:17).

First, we need to listen and respond with a purpose in our conversations. We all like to talk to others about shared interests, our families, our jobs and professions, sports, the weather, etc. But in that dialogue, are we listening? Are we seeing needs, pain, discouragement, questions, or difficulties to which we can speak? Can we discern attitudes or viewpoints that lead people away from God so we can gently help them turn back toward God?

> In humility value others above yourselves, not looking to your own interests but each of you to the interests of the others. (Philippians 2:4)

If we are genuine in our love, trustworthy in keeping confidences, and selfless in giving others the words they need to hear, the message of faith we speak will be meaningful and appreciated.

And this pertains to those outside of the church and our brothers and sisters in Christ as well. We need to love one another, minister to one another, encourage one another, and strengthen one another with the words of truth and love that Christ has provided for His church.

> Instead, speaking the truth in love, we will grow to become in every respect the mature body of him who is the head, that is, Christ. From him the whole body, joined and held together by every supporting ligament, grows and builds itself up in love, as each part does its work. (Ephesians 4:15–16)

Second, we must share our story of faith with confidence in the Spirit of God at work within us. Sometimes, we can be like Moses as he was about to lead Israel out of Egypt and doubted his ability to speak convincingly. Yet God reminded him of His presence and help.

> Please, Lord, Moses replied, I have never been eloquent, neither in the past nor since you have spoken to your servant, for I am slow of speech and tongue. And the LORD said to him, who gave man his mouth? Or who makes the mute or the deaf, the sighted or the blind? Is it not I, the LORD? Now go! I will help you as you speak, and I will teach you what to say. (Exodus 4:10–12)

We are not alone as we speak to others about Christ! We have the Holy Spirit's presence with us like God was with Moses.[3] God did not give the ministry of reconciliation to angels or reserve it for someone with the "gift" of evangelism. He gave each of us the responsibility, and if He gave us the *responsibility*, He has given us the *ability*.

All Scripture is God-breathed and is useful for teaching, rebuking, correcting and training in righteousness, so that the servant of God may be thoroughly equipped for every good work. (2 Timothy 3:16–17)

In addition to the Spirit of God at work within us, we have the word of God to make us "thoroughly equipped for every good work." That is the enablement the scriptures provide. Immersing our minds in their truth and instruction equips everyone to share their faith.

Third, our lives must reflect the godliness we speak about if we want people to take us seriously, and by default, Jesus. People don't expect perfection, but they do expect authenticity. If you tell someone you are a vegetarian, yet you eat meat, they're not going to believe you. You can loudly and with great conviction try to convince people you're a vegetarian, but they're not going to listen! And this conflict between words and actions will negate the authenticity of your message. More importantly, it diminishes the authenticity of Jesus's message. We often hear the phrase, "Be Jesus for people." But what does that really look like? You reflect Jesus when the legs of faith are evident in your lifestyle:

You live, speak, and love the truth as He did.

You unconditionally love as He did.

Your fellowship with God and unity with His people is evident and vibrant like His was.

You discipline your life to be obedient to God the Father like He did.

You can communicate your spiritually minded thoughts about the above four things in a relevant and personal way.

If these behaviors are not evident in how we try to live, no one will take our words seriously.

Our behavior validates our message.

> Do not merely listen to the word, and so deceive yourselves. Do what it says. Anyone who listens to the word but does not do what it says is like someone who looks at his face in a mirror and, after looking at himself, goes away and immediately forgets what he looks like. But whoever looks intently into the perfect law that gives freedom, and continues in it, not forgetting what they have heard, but doing it, they will be blessed in what they do. (James 1:22–25)

Remember who you are and who you are speaking and living for!

One final point here. Behind this ignorance and lack of living out our faith is a problem that I consider more deceptive and sinister. I believe that far too often, what is missing in sharing the gospel is desire. This lack of desire is the greatest hindrance to reaching out to people about it. People talk about what they love and what is most important to them. You must *want* to speak to people about the things of God. You must *want* to help people in the way you have been helped. How important is sharing the gospel to you?

Going back to chapter 4 in Exodus, the verses describing Moses's attitude about doubting God's enablement to speak to Israel should speak loudly to us.[4] Because of his unbelief, he asked God to send someone else to do what God had called him to do, which greatly angered God. God wound up sending Aaron to speak in Moses's stead. He had to cover for Moses's rebelliousness toward God's primary will. Are we guilty of this? Do we write off sharing our faith to the Missions Committee or Outreach Ministry in our church? Do we shrink in fear and turn the message of Christ over to those we deem more qualified to share it? Or is that message just not that important to us?

Often, Christians speak of how difficult it is to witness the truth of Christ in our western European and American cultures. Really? In the first through third centuries, followers of Jesus were imprisoned, tortured, burned at the stake, beheaded, and exiled. And to a lesser degree, the persecution of Christians still happens in some countries today. But the worst thing that happens to *us* is that people don't want to listen to what we have to say and sometimes become rude and insulting in response to our worldview. Actually, it has never been easier and safer to speak to people about what Christ has done for humanity, and the need for people to hear and learn about Jesus is as great as it has ever been.

Considering all the violence, desperation, hopelessness, injustice, and self-serving relative "truth" that permeates so much of this world, what more important message could there be than that given by Jesus to His disciples: "I am the way and the truth and the life. No one comes to the Father except through me."[5]

Where is our passion for speaking up? We should regularly take a deep dive into the condition of our hearts and see if there is a hole in ours about *wanting* to love others in the way that we have been loved by bringing Jesus to them.

So, how do you develop that desire?

You want to because it is part of your passion for living a godly life.

You want to because you remember what God has done for you and the story you have to tell about it.

You want to because you remember that someone else had the love and concern for your life to speak into it with the truth.

You want to because if you can recognize and speak to that hole in someone's heart, you will help him or her dramatically and potentially transform.

You want to because you are prepared to, like Peter encouraged the early church: "Always be prepared to give an answer to everyone who asks you to give the reason for the hope that you have.[6]

You want to because of who God is!

Sing to the LORD; praise his name. Each day proclaim the good news that he saves. Publish his glorious deeds among the nations. Tell everyone about the amazing things he does. Great is the LORD! He is most worthy of praise! He is to be feared above all gods. (Psalm 96:2–4)

A HOLE IN ONE

I think that when someone becomes a genuine follower of Jesus, it's a spiritual hole in one for God and His church! In the competition for winning the souls of humanity, Satan has lost another round. But it's not a game, and the consequences of losing are eternal. And it introduces a final point I want to make in this chapter.

Jesus is the way, the truth, and the life. Ironically, it is this same Jesus that stands between humanity and God. Our conversations about faith and spirituality may start with various ideas and principles about truth and purpose. That may lead to discussing the blessings of the promises of God and continue with His love and care for us. But eventually, the conversation must turn to Jesus.

So what can we say? We can say that non-Jewish people who were not trying to gain God's approval won his approval, an approval based on faith. The people of Israel tried to gain God's approval by obeying Moses's teachings, but they did not reach their goal. Why? They didn't rely on faith to gain God's approval, but they relied on their own efforts. They stumbled over the rock that trips people [Jesus Christ]. As scripture says, "I am placing a rock in Zion that people trip over, a large rock that people find offensive. Whoever believes in him will not be ashamed." (Romans 9:30–33 GWT)

This prophetic quote about the incarnation of Jesus Christ from the book of Isaiah makes the point that no matter how "religious" people are or what they believe to be a righteous and ethical standard for living, Jesus is the rock that the foundation of genuine faith is built upon. But for many, He is not a foundation for faith but an offensive obstacle in the way of how they want to live. And Satan has effectively deceived people into indifference, disregard, and even disdain for who He is.

Therefore, our evangelization efforts must eventually focus a choice of whom people will accept as their Lord. We need to recognize that we are in a spiritual battle and the urgency of the times we live in. Like my friend Jan, we need to be passionate and decisive about the message of Jesus Christ and be boldly confident in our personal ministry to share the message that God has given us.

On the pathway to godly faith, no one can successfully go around Jesus and continue the journey because Jesus is the mediator and intercessor between God and humanity. Jesus is the savior, messiah, and deliverer from sin and from our separateness from God. It is Jesus who, since first prophesied in Genesis 3 and finally arrived around four thousand years later, is the hope of humankind. It is Jesus that gave His life for the salvation of humanity. It is Jesus whom God raised from the dead to validate everything He said and was prophesied about Him. This Jesus provides the enablement for a vibrant, intimate, and consecrated faith.

> Then Jesus came to them and said, "All authority in heaven and on earth has been given to me. Therefore go and make disciples of all nations, baptizing them in the name of the Father and of the Son and of the Holy Spirit, and teaching them

to obey everything I have commanded you. And surely I am with you always, to the very end of the age." (Matthew 28:18–20 NLT)

———————

The primary message of this chapter is this: because of who Jesus is, there is no more important subject to talk about, no more loving words to speak, and no more consequential discussion to be engaged in than sharing the truth about faithfully following Him as Lord and Savior.

CHAPTER 14

THE HOPE SET BEFORE US

Seeing death as the end of life is like seeing the horizon as the end of the ocean.

—David Searls

Growing and maturing in faith is a lifelong journey. It's a journey with twists and turns, obstacles and challenges, and it can be easy and challenging. And, like constructing our faith, there will be times that we need to ask for help. It's a journey with a destination of a consecrated relationship with God. I have called it the Promised Land of Godliness. But it is not our ultimate destination.

That brings us to one final and essential aspect of faith that must always be before us. It wasn't included as one of the components in the structure of faith because it is more of a lens that we must view the whole of our faith through. It is the perspective we need our faith *in*. And, without it, we would give up.

It's called the Hope of Christ's return.

Some months after my motorcycle trip that I described in chapter 2, I had another encounter where I believe God was at work to draw me to Him. During my second year of college, I rented a room on the third floor of a large nine-bedroom house. One Friday night, there was a large and raucous dinner party. When I came home around 10:00 p.m., I was told that the party would last until two or three in the morning, and I was asked to get up early the next day to meet two men who were delivering a new refrigerator. I agreed to this, went to bed, and was up in time to open the door for them when they arrived.

After they removed the old refrigerator and installed the new one, one of the men stood in the dining room and surveyed the party's aftermath. After looking around the room, the man turned to me and said, "It looks like there was a pretty wild party here last night," to which I agreed. He then asked me a question that has stuck with me ever since: "What are you going to do when Jesus comes back?"

I don't remember my response, but I remember feeling very uncomfortable that I didn't have a meaningful answer. Any real understanding of a consequential afterlife was foreign to me at that time. I was a person who had nothing to hope for beyond this life. Answering that question has become a lifelong pursuit.

VALIDATING HOPE

The *Merriam-Webster Dictionary* defines hope as an "optimistic state of mind based on an expectation of positive outcomes concerning events and circumstances in one's life or the world at large." As a verb, its definitions include: "expect with confidence" and "to cherish a desire with anticipation."

For the most part, in everyday usage, the meaning of hope is wishful thinking about things we want to happen or achieve in this life. But hope, as defined in the scriptures, goes far beyond temporal expectations and emotional desire. And while God has given us many promises to hope for in this life, they are all centered on one tremendous and overarching eternal hope: Jesus is coming back!

> We are filled with hope, as we wait for the glorious
> return of our great God and Savior Jesus Christ.
> (Titus 2:13 CEV)

As the Bible describes, hope has always pointed people toward God's personal and experiential presence. When God initially created man and woman, they were entirely in His presence at all times. At that point, there was no need for hope because humanity was complete in every way. Ironically, their sin of trying to become *their own god* caused them to hide in fear of God. They became ashamed of who they were because even their self-identity changed to an awareness of their sin and consequential separation from Him. Because of the permanent injury that their relationship with God had sustained, they could have faced hopelessness that would have been unimaginable. But God's desire has always been to have fellowship with humanity. And He gave them hope of a time in the future when God's full presence would be restored through His redeeming them from the cause of their separation from God: sin. Throughout the Old Testament, God's people lived with a faith that looked through the lens of hope that a Messiah, the Son of God, Immanuel, or "God is with us," was coming to accomplish this.

> Therefore the Lord himself will give you a sign: The
> virgin will conceive and give birth to a son, and will
> call him Immanuel. (Isaiah 7:14)

God delivered these words of hope in different ways and over thousands of years through prophets, kings, judges, and others, as they waited in faith.[1] The fulfillment of this hope was validated when John the Baptist declared: "Look, the Lamb of God, who takes away the sin of the world ... I have seen and I testify that this is God's Chosen One"[2] (John 1:29–33).

Wherever Jesus went, His followers knew that they were in

God's presence. Because in His company were truth, love, healing, power, and forgiveness. What He said would happen did happen. What He said He would do, He did. And through His life and sacrificial death, we, too have been brought into the presence of God in the life we now live.

> But now in Christ Jesus you who once were far away have been brought near through the blood of Christ. (Ephesians 2:12–14)

The dark days between Jesus's death and before His resurrection must have been fraught with a deep sense of hopelessness for His disciples as the reality of being unable to be in His presence set in. The power of death appeared to have won. But when Jesus was resurrected from the dead, it brought a joyous, living, and real hope to His followers, then and now, that in the presence of God, even death could be overcome. The resurrection incontrovertibly certified the truth of every word Jesus said. So, as they watched Jesus ascend to the right hand of God, the angels said to them, "This same Jesus, who has been taken from you into heaven, will come back in the same way you have seen him go into heaven," they knew he would eventually return and set in order the new heaven and earth he spoke of and be with them again.[3]

We too should be convinced about the hope of Christ's return! God's message to His church is that the hope for all humanity is the Second Coming of Christ, primarily because it will fully and permanently reinstate God's presence with all people as He initially intended.

HOPE IN THIS LIFE

Sometimes it can seem like there is a giant boulder of mud floating around in the sky that indiscriminately lands on different people at different times! That can cause us to look at the world around us and question the presence of God. It can seem that God is far away or even indifferent to the human condition.[4] We can't understand all the reasons bad things happen and how they relate to the purposes of God. While we wait in hope for the return of Christ, we remain in a fallen world with bodies and minds that are compromised from God's original creation. First Corinthians 13 teaches us that our knowledge is partial. It is incomplete. Our relationship with God and who we are to Him seems like a puzzling reflection in a mirror or through a glass darkly, as the KJV puts it. While we are limited in our understanding of many things in this life, that does not mean our hope cannot be vibrant and authentic. God has given us "everything we need for a Godly life" through the "very great and precious promises" that Second Peter speaks of.

In his struggle to find the justice of God amid extreme suffering, the prophet Jeremiah wrote:

> Yet this I call to mind and therefore I have hope: Because of the Lord's great love we are not consumed, for his compassions never fail. They are new every morning; great is your faithfulness. I say to myself, "The Lord is my portion; therefore I will wait for him." (Lamentations 3:21–24)

Like those who witnessed the power of the resurrected Christ, we can see the light of God breaking through even the darkest of times and situations. Not just in the past or sometime in the future, but right now, today, we have hope to see the promises of God concerning this life come to pass.[5]

Hebrews chapter 11 reveals this through numerous lives and situations. As we build our faith through the truth that God has given us in His Word, we can face challenges like the "heroes of faith," listed here because of the hope that God keeps His promises.

Romans encourages us to be mindful of those faithful believers who came before us as examples of faith and the hope they inspire: "For whatever was written in former days was written for our instruction, that through endurance and through the encouragement of the Scriptures we might have hope" (Romans 15:4 ESV).

When we look at the lengths that God has gone to keep His word, we can trust that "our faith will be sight" and it will be "well with our souls," as the famous hymn by Horatio Spafford so beautifully speaks to our hearts.[6] When life is viewed through the hope of God's promises, we can endure through times of uncertainty, we can hurt through hope, we can grieve through hope, we can persevere through hope, and even in the darkest of times, we can have faith through hope. That's because Jesus reunited us with God spiritually in a way that made hope in the promises of God real.[7] As Peter brings to light in his first epistle: "You have not seen him, you love him; and even though you do not see him now, you believe in him and are filled with an inexpressible and glorious joy, for you are receiving the end result of your faith, the salvation of your souls" (1 Peter 1:8–9).

While Jesus is not present physically, He did not leave us alone and without the presence of God spiritually. Jesus revealed this in the Gospel of John.

> But the Advocate, the Holy Spirit, whom the Father will send in my name, will teach you all things and will remind you of everything I have said to you. (John 14:26)

> When the Advocate comes, whom I will send to you from the Father, the Spirit of truth who goes out from the Father, he will testify about me. (John 15:26)

He continues to encourage His followers in this section with some of the last words He spoke to them.

> Peace I leave with you; my peace I give you. I do not give to you as the world gives. Do not let your hearts be troubled and do not be afraid. (John 14:27)

The first epistle to the Corinthians also reminds us that God is with us through the Holy Spirit in the interim.

> But, as it is written, What no eye has seen, nor ear heard, nor the heart of man imagined, what God has prepared for those who love him, these things God has revealed to us through the Spirit.[8] (1 Corinthians 2:9)

God sent His Son to live among us, personifying truth, love, fellowship, and how to faithfully discipline our lives so that they are holy and acceptable to God and have the faith to be consecrated to Him in godliness. He showed us how to live in God's presence without the fear of rejection but in united and loving fellowship with Him and each other. He sent the comforter, the advocate, the Holy Spirit, that we might be engaged with God in a powerful and real way.

Even with all the promises for God's blessings to us in this life, there is still more to come! Our hope would be temporal at best if it were not for the return of Christ. Paul speaks to this in 1 Corinthians 15 when he wrote: "If only for this life we have hope in Christ, we are of all people most to be pitied." The completeness of our hope lies not just in this life but in the coming time of our eternal presence with God in a place where there is no grief, pain, or suffering. A place where the blessings of God are so real and rich that we are incapable of describing them. Let your mind and heart be bathed with the loving truth and comfort that the Holy Spirit has empowered us with and revealed: "Let us hold fast the confession of our hope without wavering, for he who promised is faithful (Hebrews 10:23 ESV)."

> But, as it is written, no eye has seen, nor ear heard, nor the heart of man imagined, what God has prepared for those who love him. (1 Corinthians 2:9 ESV)

> See what great love the Father has lavished on us, that we should be called children of God! And that is what we are! The reason the world does not know us is that it did not know him. Dear friends, now we are children of God, and what we will be has not yet been made known. But we know that when Christ appears, we shall be like him, for we shall see him as he is. All who have this hope in him purify themselves, just as he is. (1 John 3:1–3)

With all that God has done to draw us to Him in such a personal and meaningful way, the first epistle of Peter summarizes the proper mind-set of hope that should always be before us.

> Therefore, with minds that are alert and fully sober, set your hope on the grace to be brought to you when Jesus Christ is revealed at his coming.[9] (1 Peter 1:13)

The hope spoken of here is not defined by wishful thinking or emotions. The hope that God has called us to is a reality that we are to be spiritually minded about, just like the components of our faith—truth, love, fellowship, and the faith disciplines. How often do you think about Jesus coming back? The ramifications are sobering:

There is a grace coming like no other.

A presence of God is on the way like it was in the Garden of Eden.

An end of suffering, pain, and sorrow,

A joyous, radical, epochal, and eternal change in every aspect of life as we know it.

What a hope we have! And, like the early church, we should live with an urgency of the times because of this hope and be prepared to act on the very real possibility that Christ could return any day.

> But in your hearts honor Christ the Lord as holy, always being prepared to make a defense to anyone who asks you for a reason for the hope that is in you; yet do it with gentleness and respect. (1 Peter 3:15 ESV)

We all have a question to answer, like the man delivering the refrigerator asked me: "What are you going to do when Jesus comes back?" There are many things to prepare for as we enter each day. Are we prepared to tell others about the source of our hope? Real hope, the hope of eternal life in the personal presence of God, is something that Jesus Christ will bring to this world. It is something this world desperately needs. And Jesus has given each of His followers the authority and responsibility to put it into words to those who want to know.

———

Our faith requires hope. It inspires and energizes us to remain steadfast as we travel the path that God has laid before us and endeavor to build integrity and strength into the composition of our faith. It enables us to overcome the inevitable and sometimes seemingly insurmountable setbacks and failures that we all face at times. Our hearts' yearning grows within us as we become closer to Jesus and increasingly surrender to His will as Lord in our lives. Hope makes faith bigger than this life alone.

The important consideration of this chapter is summed up in a question: How different would your life be, and how differently would you live if the possibility of Christ's returning *today* was clearly in front of you as you travel on your journey of faith?

CHAPTER 15

FINAL WORDS

Once I finish making a chair, it is delivered to the client, and the project is complete. I probably will never see it again. I put the drawings away, file the notes, and move on to the next project. And here is where constructing the base of a chair as a metaphor for building faith ends. That's because our faith is never complete. It's always on our workbench and sits in front of us every day for our entire life. Each day, we need to stand back and put it in its intended and meaningful perspective, as well as get up close and inspect each component for integrity. We will undoubtedly need to make some changes, rework some parts, and reglue some joints. And there will be times that we need to ask for help.

For us to live in faith, we must take ownership of it. We are our own customer when it comes to building truth, love, fellowship, and discipline, and we must take ownership of our thoughts. While God is always present to inspire, energize, strengthen, and give us a living hope to help us along this process and journey, we are accountable for taking each step. The faith we build will be the basis for what we do with our lives and determine what our lives look like.

We are in charge of learning truth that governs the way we think, reason, and make conclusions about the value of faith to us.

We make a freewill choice to love in the way that God defines it.

We are tasked with building genuine fellowship with God and His church rather than superficial relations.

We are responsible for developing disciplined habits of spiritual formation.

We take control of our thoughts to align with the mind of Christ and the interrelationship of the legs of our faith.

As our faith continues to deepen and mature, it will change the appearance of the life we build upon it. It will change to reflect Jesus:

like the rancher who spoke into my life about my spiritual direction

like my father when he showed such kindness and forgiveness when I damaged his car

like the mentor I had as an apprentice who with patience and wisdom helped me become the artisan I wanted to be

like the man delivering the refrigerator who used a life situation to bring Jesus into the conversation

and like countless other people that you and I have known who genuinely demonstrate their faith as evidenced by the fruit of the spirit they manifest

> But what happens when we live God's way? He brings gifts into our lives, much the same way that fruit appears in an orchard—things like affection for others, exuberance about life, serenity. We develop a willingness to stick with things, a sense of compassion in the heart, and a conviction that a basic holiness permeates things and people. We find ourselves involved in loyal commitments, not needing to force our way in life, able to marshal and direct our energies wisely. (Galatians 5:22–23 Message)

God made a covenant with Israel in Moab as they were about to enter the promised land of Canaan. Despite the time they had wasted in disobedience to Him, and their numerous episodes of hard heartedness, sin, and even idolatry, He never forsook them, even though at many times they had forsaken Him. And, like Israel, God is always with us despite the times we may have turned from Him and wandered off the path of our journey of faith. The promises He made to Israel He has surely made to us through Christ.

> Now what I am commanding you today is not too difficult for you or beyond your reach. It is not up in heaven, so that you have to ask, "Who will ascend into heaven to get it and proclaim it to us so we may obey it?" Nor is it beyond the sea, so that you have to ask, "Who will cross the sea to get it and proclaim it to us so we may obey it?" No, the word is very near you; it is in your mouth and in your heart so you may obey it. See, I set before you today life and prosperity, death and destruction. For I command you today to love the LORD your God, to walk in obedience to him, and to keep his commands, decrees and laws; then you will live and increase, and the LORD your God will bless you in the land you are entering to possess. (Deuteronomy 30:11–16)

The qualities, purposes, and outcomes of our lives are determined by which words we choose to live by. My prayer for you, and one I would hope that you pray for me, is that we would choose to follow God's directions on our journey of faith. That we would not wander from the path with worldly values and enticements, turn around to head back to the slavery of unbelief, or lose sight of the destination. And that we would never settle for a faith that is "good enough."

If I could provide a benediction over what has been presented in this book, it would be this:

through the truth that God has given us in His word,

through the love He has shown us through Christ,

through the intimate fellowship we can have with Him and His church,

through our personal dedication and faithfulness to practice the disciplines of spiritual formation,

through committing ourselves to loving God with our minds by thinking like Jesus,

through the hope set before us of the eternal presence of God and knowing Him like He knows us,

through the power of the Holy Spirit, and with the enablements that God has given us,

let us be faithful and intentional in constructing an unshakeable faith and dedicate the purpose of our lives to reflect the inspired words of Henry Varley: "The world has yet to see what God can do with and for and through and in a man [or woman] who is fully and wholly consecrated to Him."

AFTERWORD

During the year and a half that I spent writing this book, my wife of forty-two years was in the process of dying. She passed away the week after I began sending out my final draft for publication. One might ask how I could possibly be writing a book during such an emotionally draining and potentially faith-challenging time. I wanted to address this in this afterword because I have learned some things about faith through this part of my journey that otherwise I may have never grasped. And I hope that what I share will help others who have encountered very difficult challenges like this on their faith journey.

First, I learned something that I never expected—that individual freedom and independence can turn into self-serving values. And when pursued at all costs, they can even become idols that numb our humanity. Additionally, zealous independence and unrestrained freedom can often be a cover for fear. Fear of responsibility, commitment, and accountability. It was through the loss of much of my personal freedom and independence due to the need of taking care of my wife that sacrificing them for her good became liberating and fulfilling! There can be transformational fulfillment in sacrificing something you value for the good of someone else. And in our American culture, freedom and independence are some of our most guarded and valued privileges. However, true freedom and independence come from selfless giving and self-sacrifice because we cut loose of being so concerned with the burden of doing what we want, and we begin focusing on the needs of others. We become liberated from the burden of always focusing on and pleasing ourselves!

More importantly, I learned that even when we are amid life's most challenging and painful circumstances, we can guard and persevere in faith, and persist in doing the things that keep our faith intentionally in front of us at all times. When our life circumstances are at their worst, our pursuit of faith can be at its best. Our faith is what will carry us through life's dark tunnels and into the light again and will give us the perspective we need to be patient and courageous. Writing this book was the touchstone for faith that I needed for that perspective and eventually opened my eyes to one of the most important lessons about faith I have experienced so far: what unconditional love really means.

When we married, I made a vow to always love my wife. I took it seriously. For decades, I would ask God to show me how to love my wife in a way that was meaningful and helpful to her. Over those years, I pictured the way I loved her in a certain context. Like the way I spoke to her, encouraged her when she needed it, and doing things together that she enjoyed. It included raising our family, the ways I could help her around the house, traveling together, and working together to help others. My picture of loving her also included enjoying our hobbies and pastimes together, as well as in our love life.

However, that context changed dramatically when she got sick. There was no more travel. There were no more activities together the way they used to be. But I had still vowed to love her through sickness and health, and I meant to keep it. When I made that vow at age twenty-six, I pictured sickness like a bad cold or broken leg. A terminal illness was totally off my radar screen. The circumstances in which I loved her went from a relationship with a winsome and sophisticated woman to that of a helpless child needing around-the-clock care.

But I kept my vow. Through the help of her doctors, the encouragement and support of some dear friends, and especially the involvement of my sister and my daughter, I was able to dot every "I" and cross every "T" in loving her in the way I know that Christ would have me do it. I look back on that time with no guilt, doubts, or anger. And I've learned some things from this experience that have been transformative and made me a better person.

It has become clear to me that to carry out the command to love, we often need others to help us learn to love in circumstances that are unfamiliar, painful, or even overwhelming. I used to think that loving people was something I had to do on my own. And while truly it starts with a personal choice to do so, sometimes we need help. Getting help to love unconditionally relieves us of the burdens of doing it alone and often less effectively!

What is important is that we do whatever we must to love, and we can! God would not command us to do something that is impossible. And I think He has made it necessary for us to reach out to others at times for help. It is always possible for us to love unconditionally.

And in the context of what is written in this book: "And if I have a faith that can move mountains, but do not have love, I am nothing (1 Corinthians 13:2b)."

APPENDIX 1

CHAPTER BOOKENDS

Each chapter has opened with a relative quote (reference noted in the chapter) and closed with something for you to consider about faith. They are listed here as a reference for contemplation.

Chapter 1: Changing Direction

Quote: Nothing whatever, whether great or small, can happen to a believer, without God's ordering and permission. There is no such thing as "chance," "luck" or "accident" in the Christian's journey through this world. All is arranged and appointed by God. And all things are "working together" for the believer's good.

Consideration: What do your thoughts about God tell you about the direction of your faith?

Chapter 2: The Promised Land of Godliness

Quote: The Christian experience, from start to finish, is a journey of faith.

Consideration: Is what you believe, value, and trust pointing you toward Egypt or Canaan?

Chapter 3: The Picture of Faith

Quote: *To one who has faith, no explanation is necessary. To one without faith, no explanation is possible.*

Consideration: Your life can be a picture of genuine, godly faith. Take your faith in God seriously. Value and guard it. Make the effort to understand and grow in it. Make it your life's priority.

Chapter 4: The Structure of Faith

Quote: The secret of change is to focus all your energy not on fighting the old but on building the new.

Consideration: There is a real and understandable structure for our journey of faith that provides us with accurate directions and measurable progress. It is composed of truth, love, fellowship, the faith disciplines, and being spiritually minded.

Chapter 5: Assessing Faith

Quote: Examine yourselves to see if your faith is genuine. Test yourselves.

Consideration: Even more important than the time and effort we spend assessing our health, finances, personal goals, and so many other areas of our life, understanding and stewarding our faith needs constant attention. With God's help, the support of our church family, and pure-hearted engagement on our part, our faith can be nurtured into maturity.

Chapter 6: The Leg of Truth

Quote: To risk reputation and affection for the truth's sake is so demanding that to do it constantly you will need a degree of moral principle that only the Spirit of God can work in you.

Consideration: Truth is the blueprint for building faith.

Chapter 7: The Leg of Love

Quote: God bestows His blessings without discrimination. The followers of Jesus are children of God, and they should manifest the family likeness by doing good to all, even to those who deserve the opposite.

Consideration: The need to receive as well as give love is a foundational need of human existence. Choosing to love the way God defines it and in the way that Jesus lived it fulfills this need and empowers us to pursue and manifest the faith of Jesus Christ.

Chapter 8: The Leg of Fellowship

Quote: Anyone who measures Christlikeness only in terms of growth in his or her fellowship with God takes an incomplete measurement. Spiritual maturity also includes growth in fellowship with the children of God.

Consideration: Watch over and care for your fellowship with God and His church in the same way that you watch over and care for your life. Your faith cannot support your life without it.

Chapter 9: The Leg of the Faith Disciplines

Quote: Translate your dreams of spiritual growth into concrete patterns of behavior that God has designed to promote your spiritual progress.

Consideration: Do not be deceived: God cannot be mocked. A man reaps what he sows.

Chapter 10: The Stretcher of Being Spiritually Minded

Quote: Watch your thoughts, they become your words; watch your words, they become your actions; watch your actions, they become your habits; watch your habits, they become your character; watch your character, it becomes your destiny.

Consideration: It's not just words on a page we are setting our minds upon; it is the Lord Himself.

Chapter 11: Building Five Habits for Being Spiritually Minded

Quote: Habit is the intersection of knowledge (what to do), skill (how to do), and desire (want to do).

Consideration: If you remain in me and my words remain in you, ask whatever you wish, and it will be done for you. This is to my Father's glory, that you bear much fruit, showing yourselves to be my disciples.

Chapter 12: Assembling Faith

Quote: A life of reaction is a life of slavery, intellectually and spiritually. One must fight for a life of action, not reaction.

Consideration: While you are responsible for constructing your faith, you are not alone. You have the Father, the Son, and the Holy Spirit as well as your brothers and sisters in Christ to ensure your faith is genuine.

Chapter 13: Sharing Faith

Quote: Our faith becomes stronger as we express it; a growing faith is a sharing faith.

Consideration: Because of who Jesus is, there is no more important subject to talk about, no more loving words to speak, and no more consequential discussion to be engaged in, than sharing the truth about faithfully following Him as our Lord and Savior.

Chapter 14: The Hope Set Before Us:

Quote: Seeing death as the end of life is like seeing the horizon as the end of the ocean.

Consideration: How different would your life be and how differently would you live if the possibility of Christ's returning *today* was clearly in front of you as you travel on your journey of faith?

APPENDIX 2

FAITH ASSESSMENTS

It's important that we spend some time alone with God in deep surrender to His will, honest conversation about our faith, and solitary and quiet listening to what He is whispering to our souls. Men and women of God have done this for centuries. Not just by being a recluse or sequestering ourselves to a life of isolation. God needs us out in the culture speaking the truth and loving people, spreading the good news of Jesus Christ, and helping people become His followers and disciples. But He needs us to do it with confidence in who we are to Him and conviction about our message. Spending some quiet time in isolation to evaluate the sincerity of our faith and learning where we need to change and grow can invigorate and refresh our souls, not only for our spiritual formation but for becoming clear and convinced about our role in His work.

I want to explain two methods of evaluating your faith that have been very helpful to me over the years. They have been helpful to me to shape a format for what I want to accomplish during this special time with God. You may need to modify them to suit your schedule, resources, and needs but I believe that if you follow their basic structure, they will be a tremendous help in deepening the meaning of your faith and practice of a spiritual life.

The first one involves a frequent practice of spiritual introspection that can take under an hour. I call it a faith checkup. The second entails getting isolated for at least a day or two and taking a deeper dive into our spiritual condition. This I call a faith assessment retreat.

A FAITH CHECKUP

The purpose of a faith checkup is to keep our spiritual growth in front of us as a priority and pursuit. We should never let a week go by without checking in on our spiritual health. It is part of stewarding the life that God has given us and follows the exhortation given in Philippians to "Work hard to show the results of your salvation, obeying God with deep reverence and fear."

I propose a weekly time, maybe an hour or so, of prayer, meditation, confession, and evaluation of the direction our faith is headed. It could also be effective as part of your daily devotional time. Here are five ideas that are helpful to me on how to do this.

Get up before everyone else and go to an isolated and quiet place in your home where you won't be disturbed. I'm an early riser, so a predawn time works for me. I like the stillness of the early morning and not having had to engage my brain in much for the day ahead yet. Whatever time and place you choose, what is important is that you have a quiet place where you will not be disturbed and can clear your mind of distractions.

Meditate on one scripture that really speaks to you about what God thinks of you, the person He wants you to be, or wants you to do with your life. The way I do this is to read the entire verse over and over a few times, sometimes out loud, and then focus on specific sections or words. What do they mean *to me*? What is God saying *to me*? Can I insert *my name* in the context? If you memorize or write down the verse, you can carry it with you throughout the week and regularly refresh your thoughts with it.

Bring your faith before God in a conversation with Him. Imagine

Jesus standing in front of you with His hands on your shoulders and looking straight into your eyes as you talk to Him. You have His full attention. Feel the strength and warmth of His hands, hear His breathing as He is so close, and see the kind yet penetrating gaze of His eyes. Experience the security and sobriety of His presence!

Check your heart. Are you at peace with God? Is your attitude about your faith pleasing to God? If not, identify the cause and confess it to Him. Remember, He is right there with you. Ask for forgiveness if you need it and for His help. Honestly lay those deep concerns before Him. When I am not at peace with God, it is difficult to be at peace about anything. Clear this up with Him before you go into your day.

Pray over the five components of faith and say that you will live them out today and throughout the week:

Truth
Love
Fellowship
The faith disciplines
Being spiritually minded

As you practice all or some of these on a regular basis, you will come to cherish this time with your Heavenly Father and with His Son. It will help to keep you on the path of godliness and progressing on your journey of faith.

A FAITH ASSESSMENT RETREAT

The purpose of a faith assessment retreat is to take whatever time is needed to dig deeply into the condition of your heart, enrich your relationship with God, honestly evaluate your faith, and make some concrete plans for spiritual growth. It involves blocking out some time once a year to get away in solitude. Somewhere quiet and isolated from all distractions. It may be at a cabin in the mountains, a quiet hotel by the ocean, a friend's house that is unoccupied, or a tent in the woods. The location doesn't matter, if it works.

Your retreat may be for just a couple of days or much longer. It's a time to intentionally put into practice apostle Paul's exhortation to the believers in Galatia, to "take off your old self with its practices and put on the new self, which is being renewed in knowledge in the image of its Creator."

The following suggestions come from my experience in doing this. What you do may vary, but what is important is to put some thought, planning, and purpose into this special time. It can be transformative and something you look forward to each year.

Prepare beforehand:

It's important that you make physical preparations for your retreat:

Organize your schedule so that your family or work will not need to interrupt you.

Avoid electronics that will interrupt or distract your purpose for being there. Leave them at home or in your car.

Plan your meals, drinks, snacks, and supplies so you have everything you need and don't need to go out to eat, shop, or run errands.

It's also important to make some spiritual preparations for your retreat:

Write down a few important purposes for your retreat. Are there areas of your faith you need to discuss with Him? Is there a verse of scripture or a particular idea that defines a theme for you retreat? Having a theme for my retreat has been particularly helpful to me. Humility, trusting and surrendering to the will of God, and the wisdom of God are themes that I have used.

Pray over your upcoming time to be what God wants it to be.

Ask others to be in prayer for you while you are there.

Perhaps begin or end your retreat by fasting.

Aside from your physical needs, all you must bring with you is a Bible, notepad, and pencil. You don't really need any other books. You are not there to read about faith; you are there to talk to God and listen to God about *your* faith.

Settle in.

Once you are settled in physically, get settled in spiritually:

Sit quietly, take some deep breaths, and listen to the silence for a while.

Be aware that God is with you. Picture Jesus in the room with you, or if you're outside, sitting or walking next to you.

You're not in a hurry.

Open your retreat with prayer:

Speak to God, with thankfulness for His love for you.

Ask Him for forgiveness of your sins, and ask that you would begin this time together free of all distractions and concerns, and focus on this time together with Him.

Ask for God to give you a pure and humble heart that is receptive and sensitive to His presence and guidance, whatever that may be.

Ask God to empower you with confidence in His strength to become the man or woman He has called you to be.

Lay your life before Him.

Remember to be thankful for the faith you have and the ways that God has blessed you!

You're not in a hurry.

Continue your time by reading the word of God.

Be mindful that "it's not just the words on a page we are setting our minds upon; it is the Lord himself." Consider the words of Randy Harris from *Soul Work*:

I have come to believe that there is only one really serious Bible study question and that is "If I took this text seriously, what would have to change?" And the most important Bible study skill is not learning to read Greek, although that is an important skill. The most important skill in studying scripture is a willingness to listen, to allow scripture to call us into question, and to invite us into change.

God talks to us through His word and in prayer. He knows why you're doing this and what you need. Let Him speak to you and listen to what He says.

You're not in a hurry.

Take an honest look at the condition of your faith.

Perhaps a good way to start this is by evaluating the quality of the components of faith written about in this book. The answers don't all have to be negative! But ask yourself where you need to have more understanding and growth in these areas:

Truth
Love of God and people
Fellowship with God and His Church
The faith disciplines
Being spiritually minded

Another avenue of introspection that helps you understand the quality of your faith is the degree of the fruit of the spirit in your life as outlined in Galatians.

> But the Holy Spirit produces this kind of fruit in our lives: love, joy, peace, patience, kindness, goodness, faithfulness, gentleness, and self-control. There is no law against these things! (Galatians 5:22–23)

Honestly evaluate where your location is on your journey of faith in relation to these qualities of godliness. Write down what you discover and conclude about what needs to change.

CONSIDER THE THRESHOLDS

Chapter 11 listed five thresholds that can be used to give you a general idea as to where you are on your journey of faith. This is an excellent time to examine where you are on the continuum of spiritual formation. They can tell your current location and where you need to be headed. There are no right or wrong answers. Make sure to be thankful you have come as far as you have!

LOOK FOR ELEPHANTS

You don't even need to look for them; you already know what they are! Those big obstacles that continue to be hindrances to your faith that don't seem to ever leave the room. They usually are connected in some way to an absence, rejection, misunderstanding, or ignorance of the five components of faith discussed in this book. This connection may be deeply imbedded in our psyche from childhood, a tragic incident, weakness of character, or even bad theology. If they seem too difficult to handle on your own, that's fine; they are! That's why you're doing this! Because no matter how big the obstacle, God is bigger!

> I have found that some of my "elephants" cannot be completely resolved immediately but can take time. You're probably familiar with the saying that the way to eat an elephant is one bite at a time. If your time on your retreat enables you to take only one or two bites, you are successful. More will come as you stay faithful. We can take comfort and be reassured that God is more than able to help us when we remember these words of our Lord: "But Jesus beheld them, and said unto them, with

men this is impossible; but with God all things are possible" (Matthew 19:26).

You're not in a hurry.
Discuss what you find with your Heavenly Father.
You're not going to surprise Him! As Psalm 139:1–4 lovingly reveals:

> You have searched me, LORD, and you know me. You know when I sit and when I rise; you perceive my thoughts from afar. You discern my going out and my lying down; you are familiar with all my ways. Before a word is on my tongue you, LORD, know it completely.

Lay your challenges about faith before Him with trust and humility, and ask Him for help, strength, wisdom, and guidance.

Especially, talk with Him about how you're going to start eating those elephants! What will the first bite be?

Write down what he shows you.

You're not in a hurry.

Take a break and then continue the same pattern.

Do something to refresh yourself like taking a walk, having a meal or snack, or even a short nap, but then get back at it. Allow yourself to be flexible. During one of my retreats, I remember waking up at three one morning, getting dressed, and going for a walk. They sky was clear with a beautiful moon, and the stillness of the night reminded me to "be still and know that I am God." I walked out into this huge field, sat down on a tree stump, and for the next hour had one of the most meaningful and transformational discussions I have ever had with God. Your observations will change, your questions will change, your prayers to and discussions with God will change, but with every cycle of this practice, you will go deeper into the will of God for your life. He will open your eyes to what you need to do and how you need to change.

You're not in a hurry.

Go deeper.

Write a short list of the things you value the most and why.

Ask yourself if they have the same value to God, and ask how you know this.

Ask yourself if you are willing to prioritize them to align with God's will.

Are you satisfied with the direction and progress of your spiritual life?

What is working and what is not?

In what ways are you becoming more like Jesus in the way you live?

In what ways are they reflected in your behavior?

What do you need to learn, and what behavior do you need to change?

What are the most challenging obstacles you face in your spiritual maturity?

Are there elephants on the path? If so, define them here.

What will you do to overcome them?

Do you need to talk to and get help from someone about this, and who would you trust to do this?

What would you consider to be the three main obstacles you face on your journey of faith?

You may need to change some of the questions to be more consequential to you, but what's important is that you do it in a meaningful, honest, and soul-searching way. What you learn here will enlighten you to the changes you need to make to your spiritual diet and exercise. And what is important is what we decide to do about the information.

And, of course, you're not in a hurry!

Close your retreat event in prayer and with a plan.

As you finish your time of assessment, write down what you

have learned that you need to do differently. List the changes you are going to make and when you are going to make them. Develop a plan to follow up on your progress. Your faith checkup practice will be an excellent time for this. Thank God for the time you have spent, what you have learned, and ask for His help in the changes and plans you have made. This is part of what Paul told Timothy when he encouraged him to "train yourself to be godly."

If you have been intentional and faithful to conscientiously follow this process in this time of "waiting upon the lord," you will complete your retreat with renewed vision and strength for moving forward on your journey of faith. You will walk away leaving some obstacles behind you, taking some answers with you, and be clear on some plans. Most importantly, your fellowship with God will be sweeter and stronger, and you'll be more sensitive to the influence of His spirit within you.

> But they that wait upon the LORD shall renew their strength; they shall mount up with wings as eagles; they shall run, and not be weary; and they shall walk, and not faint. (Isaiah 40:31)

APPENDIX 3

CHAPTER NOTES AND HELPFUL SCRIPTURES

Introduction

1   Excerpt from *Red Sister*, by Mark Lawrence, Ace Books, 2017.
2   Irving Stone, *The Agony and the Ecstasy*, Doubleday, 1961.
3   Excerpt from *Everyone's a Theologian: An Introduction to Systematic Theology*, by R. C. Sproul, Reformation Trust Publishing, 2014.

Chapter 1: Changing Direction

1   R. C. Sproul (1939–2017) was a Presbyterian minister and founder of Liginier Ministries. He was one of the most influential popularizers of Reformed theology spanning the late twentieth and early twenty-first centuries.
2   Excerpt from *The Complete Works of Lao Tzu: Tao Teh Ching & Hau Hu Ching*, by Lao Tzu, Tao of Wellness Press, 1995.
3   Additional scriptures relative to our journey to the Promised land of Godliness include:

(All scriptures quoted are from the Eastern Standard Version)

"Prove me, O LORD, and try me; test my heart and my mind" (Psalm 26:2 ESV).

"When I think on my ways, I turn my feet to your testimonies" (Psalm 119:59 ESV).

"In all your ways acknowledge him, and he will make straight your paths" (Proverbs 3:6 ESV).

"Let us test and examine our ways, and return to the LORD!" (Lamentations 3:40 ESV).

"Examine yourselves, to see whether you are in the faith. Test yourselves. Or do you not realize this about yourselves, that Jesus Christ is in you?—unless indeed you fail to meet the test!" (2 Corinthians 13:5 ESV).

"For if anyone thinks he is something, when he is nothing, he deceives himself. But let each one test his own work, and then his reason to boast will be in himself alone and not in his neighbor. For each will have to bear his own load" (Galatians 6:3–5 ESV).

"But test everything; hold fast what is good" (1 Thessalonians 5:21 ESV).

Chapter 2: The Promised Land of Godliness

1   "After leaving Sukkoth they camped at Etham on the edge of the desert. By day the LORD went ahead of them in a pillar of cloud to guide them on their way and by night in a pillar of fire to give them light, so that they could travel by day or night. Neither the pillar of cloud by day nor the pillar of fire by night left its place in front of the people" (Exodus 13:20–22).

2   Excerpt from *Self Reliance,* by Ralph Waldo Emerson, 1841.

3   *The Principle of the Path: How to Get from Where You Are to Where You Want to Be,* by Andy Stanley.

4   Additional scriptures relative to our journey to the Promised land of Godliness include:

(All scriptures quoted are from the Eastern Standard Version)

"This Book of the Law shall not depart from your mouth, but you shall meditate on it day and night, so that you may be careful to do according to all that is written in it. For then you will make your way prosperous, and then you will have good success (Joshua 1:8 ESV)."

"They refused to obey and were not mindful of the wonders that you performed among them, but they stiffened their neck and appointed a leader to return to their slavery in Egypt. But you are a God ready to forgive, gracious and merciful, slow to anger and abounding in steadfast love, and did not forsake them" (Nehemiah 9:17 ESV).

"Blessed is the man who walks not in the counsel of the wicked, nor stands in the way of sinners, nor sits in the seat of scoffers; but his delight is in the law of the Lord, and on his law he meditates day and night. He is like a tree planted by streams of water that yields its fruit in its season, and its leaf does not wither. In all that he does, he prospers" (Psalm 1:1–3 ESV).

"I bless the Lord who gives me counsel; in the night also my heart instructs me. I have set the Lord always before me; because he is at my right hand, I shall not be shaken" (Psalm 16:7–8 ESV).

"He restores my soul. He leads me in paths of righteousness for his name's sake (Psalm 23:3 ESV).

"Make me to know your ways, O Lord; teach me your paths" (Psalm 25:4 ESV).

"He leads the humble in what is right, and teaches the humble his way" (Psalm 25:9 ESV).

The steps of a man are established by the Lord, when he delights in his way; though he fall, he shall not be cast headlong, for the Lord upholds his hand (Psalm 37:23–24 ESV).

"When I think on my ways, I turn my feet to your testimonies" (Psalm 119:59 ESV).

"But the path of the righteous is like the light of dawn, which shines brighter and brighter until full day" (Proverbs 4:18 ESV).

"Whoever walks with the wise becomes wise, but the companion of fools will suffer harm. Disaster pursues sinners, but the righteous are rewarded with good" (Proverbs 13:20–21 ESV).

Thus says the LORD, your Redeemer, the Holy One of Israel: "I am the LORD your God, who teaches you to profit, who leads you in the way you should go. Oh that you had paid attention to my commandments! Then your peace would have been like a river, and your righteousness like the waves of the sea" (Isaiah 48:17–18 ESV).

"For I know the plans I have for you, declares the LORD, plans for welfare and not for evil, to give you a future and a hope (Jeremiah 29:11 ESV)"

"For we walk by faith, not by sight" (2 Corinthians 5:7 ESV).

"Look carefully then how you walk, not as unwise but as wise" (Ephesians 5:15 ESV).

Chapter 3: The Picture of Faith

1   Irving Stone, *The Agony and the Ecstasy*, Doubleday, NY, 1961.
2   More information on the history of this fallacy can be found online at The Conversation.com,

"Why you should know about the New Thought movement," by Christopher H. Evans, February 15, 2017.

3   Excerpt from *Dealing with Doubt*, by Greg Laurie at the Harvest.org website, November 13, 2010.
4   Excerpt from *God in the Dark*, by Os Guiness, Crossway, 1996.
5   "Then Jesus said to Thomas, put your finger here and look at My hands. Reach out your hand and put it into my side. Stop doubting and believe. Thomas replied, 'My Lord and my God!' (John 20: 27–28)."

6   "I have told you these things, so that in me you may have peace. In this world you will have trouble. But take heart! I have overcome the world." (John 16:33)

7   "For you formed my inward parts; you knitted me together in my mother's womb. I praise you, for I am fearfully and wonderfully made. Wonderful are your works; my soul knows it very well" (Psalm 139:13–14).

"No, in all these things we are more than conquerors through him who loved us. For I am sure that neither death nor life, nor angels nor rulers, nor things present nor things to come, nor powers, nor height nor depth, nor anything else in all creation, will be able to separate us from the love of God in Christ Jesus our Lord" (Romans 8:37–39).

8   "Looking to Jesus, the founder and perfecter of our faith, who for the joy that was set before him endured the cross, despising the shame, and is seated at the right hand of the throne of God" (Hebrews 12:2).

Chapter 4: The Structure of Faith

1   German-born architect Ludwig Mies van der Rohe (1886–1969) in a February 1957 article in *Time* magazine about furniture designed by architects.
2   "Therefore everyone who hears these words of mine and puts them into practice is like a wise man who built his house on the rock. The rain came down, the streams rose, and the winds blew and beat against that house; yet it did not fall, because it had its foundation on the rock. But everyone who hears these words of mine and does not put them into practice is like a foolish man who built his house on sand. The rain came down, the streams rose, and the winds blew and beat against that house, and it fell with a great crash" (Matthew 7:24–27).

"By the grace God has given me, I laid a foundation as a wise builder, and someone else is building on it. But each one should build with care. For no one can lay any foundation other than the one already laid, which is Jesus Christ" (1 Corinthians 3:10–11).

"Yet you, Lord, are our Father. We are the clay, you are the potter; we are all the work of your hand" (Isaiah 64:8).

3   Excerpt from, "Form of the Good,", by Plato, outlined in *1000 Word Philosophy, An Introduction to Anthology*, February 13, 2018.

Chapter 5: Assessing Our Faith

1   Kristen Wetherell is the author of *Fight Your Fears: Trusting God's Character and Promises When You Are Afraid*, coauthor of the award-winning book *Hope When It Hurts: Biblical Reflections to Help You Grasp God's Purpose in Your Suffering"*; she blogs at setapart.net.
2   The Gospel Coalition is a fellowship of evangelical churches in the Reformed tradition and can be found on the web at: https://www.thegospelcoalition.org. The quote is an excerpt from an article entitled, "Don't Be Introspective. Examine Yourself," by Kristen Wetherell, July 19, 2018.
3   "Draw near to God, and he will draw near to you. Cleanse your hands, you sinners, and purify your hearts, you double-minded" (James 4:8 ESV).

"Let us draw near with a true heart in full assurance of faith, with our hearts sprinkled clean from an evil conscience and our bodies washed with pure water" (Hebrews 10:22 ESV).

"Create in me a clean heart, O God, and renew a right spirit within me" (Psalm 51:10 ESV).

"Trust in the Lord with all your heart, and do not lean on your own understanding. In all your ways acknowledge him, and he will make straight your paths. Be not wise in your own eyes; fear the Lord and turn away from evil. It will be healing to your flesh and refreshment to your bones" (Proverbs 3:5–8 ESV).

"Search me, O God, and know my heart! Try me and know my thoughts! And see if there be any grievous way in me, and lead me in the way everlasting! (Psalm 139:23–24 ESV).

4   "Keep (guard) your heart with all vigilance, for from it flow the springs of life" (Proverbs 4:23 ESV).

5   These thresholds have been excerpted from and expanded upon from the book, *Move, What 1,000 Churches Reveal About Spiritual Growth,* by Greg L. Hawkins and Cally Parkinson, Zondervan Press, 2011.

Chapter 6: The Leg of Truth

1   "'You are a king, then!' said Pilate. Jesus answered, 'You say that I am a king. In fact, the reason I was born and came into the world is to testify to the truth. Everyone on the side of truth listens to me.' 'What is truth?' retorted Pilate" (John 18:37–38).

2   Excerpt from, "Love Must Mature," article on Bible.org, June 10, 2004, by Greg Herrick, project director for KnowingGod.org.

"Do your best to present yourself to God as one approved, a worker who has no need to be ashamed, rightly handling the word of truth" (2 Timothy 2:15 ESV).

"I have no greater joy than to hear that my children are walking in the truth" (3 John 1:4 ESV).

3   "If anyone thinks they are something when they are not, they deceive themselves" (Galatians 6:3 ESV).

"I suspect you would never intend this, but this is what happens. When you attempt to live by your own religious plans and projects, you are cut off from Christ, you fall out of grace (Galatians 5:4–6, Message Bible).

4   "Your word is a lamp to my feet and a light to my path" (Psalm 119:105 ESV).

The sum of your word is truth, and every one of your righteous rules endures forever" (Psalm 119:160 (ESV).

"Every word of God proves true; he is a shield to those who take refuge in him" (Proverbs 30:5 ESV).

5   Excerpt from rollsoffthetongue.tumblr.com.

"I have revealed you to those whom you gave me out of the world. They were yours; you gave them to me and they have obeyed your word. Now they know that everything you have given me comes from you. For I gave them the words you gave me and they accepted them. They knew with certainty that I came from you, and they believed that you sent me (John 17:6–8 ESV).

6   "The Lord is near to all who call on Him, to all who call out to Him in truth" (Psalm 145:18).

Chapter 7: The Leg of Love

1   Walter C. Kaiser Jr., Peter H. Davids, F. F. Bruce, Manfred Brauch (2010), *Hard Sayings of the Bible*, 366, InterVarsity Press.

2   "For I am convinced that neither death nor life, neither angels nor principalities, neither the present nor the future, nor any powers, neither height nor depth, nor anything else in all creation, will be able to separate us from the love of God that is in Christ Jesus our Lord" (Romans 8:38–39).

3   "For we do not have a high priest who is unable to empathize with our weaknesses, but we have one who has been tempted in every way, just as we are yet he did not sin (Hebrews 4:15).

4   "You were taught, with regard to your former way of life, to put off your old self, which is being corrupted by its deceitful desires; to be made new in the attitude of your minds; and to put on the new self, created to be like God in true righteousness and holiness" (Ephesians 4:24).

5   "Dear friends, let us love one another, for love comes from God. Everyone who loves has been born of God and knows God. Whoever does not love does not know God, because God is love" (1 John 4:7–8).

6   "Love is patient, love is kind. It does not envy, it does not boast, it is not proud. It does not dishonor others, it is not self-seeking, it is not easily angered, it keeps no record of wrongs. Love does not delight in evil but rejoices with the truth. It always protects, always trusts, always hopes, always perseveres. Love never fails (1 Corinthians 13:4–8).

7   "A new command I give you: Love one another. As I have loved you, so you must love one another. By this everyone will know that you are my disciples, if you love one another" (John 13:34–35).

8   "He doesn't want to destroy anyone but wants all people to have an opportunity to turn to him and change the way they think and act" (2 Peter 3:9 GWT).

"This is good, and pleases God our Savior, who wants all people to be saved and to come to a knowledge of the truth. For there is one God and one mediator between God and mankind, the man Christ Jesus, who gave himself as a ransom for all people" (1 Timothy 2:3–6).

9   "This is how God showed his love among us: He sent his one and only Son into the world that we might live through him. This is love: not that we loved God, but that he loved us and sent his Son as an atoning sacrifice for our sins" (1 John 4:9–10).

10   "But God demonstrates his own love for us in this: While we were still sinners, Christ died for us. For if, while we were God's enemies, we were reconciled to him through the death of his Son, how much more, having been reconciled, shall we be saved through his life!" (Romans 5:8, 10).

"You're familiar with the old written law, 'Love your friend,' and its unwritten companion, 'Hate your enemy.' I'm challenging that. I'm telling you to love your enemies. Let them bring out the best in you, not the worst. When someone gives you a hard time, respond with the energies of prayer, for then you are working out of your true selves, your God-created selves. This is what God does. He gives his best, the sun to warm and the rain to nourish, to everyone, regardless: the good and bad, the nice and nasty. If all you do is love the lovable, do you expect a bonus? Anybody can do that. If you simply say hello to those who greet you, do you expect a medal? Any run-of-the-mill sinner does that. In a word, what I'm saying is, grow up. You're kingdom subjects. Now live like it. Live out your God-created identity. Live generously and graciously toward others, the way God lives toward you" (Matthew 5:43–48, Message).

11   Excerpt from *The Epistles of St. Peter*, by John Henry Jowett, New Century Books, 2010.

12   "For God so loved the world that He gave His one and only Son, that everyone who believes in Him shall not perish but have eternal life" (John 3:16).

13　Excerpt from *Clarke's Commentary: The Holy Bible Containing the Old and New Testaments with a Commentary and Critical Notes*, vol. 6, by Adam Clarke, Abingdon Press, publication date unknown. Adam Clarke (1762–1832) was a British Methodist theologian and biblical scholar. He is chiefly remembered for writing a commentary on the Bible, which took him forty years to complete and which was a primary Methodist theological resource for two centuries.

14　"Love the Lord your God with all your heart and with all your soul and with all your mind and with all your strength. The second is this: Love your neighbor as yourself. There is no commandment greater than these" (Mark 12:30–31).

15　"So that Christ may dwell in your hearts through faith—that you, being rooted and grounded in love, may have strength to comprehend with all the saints what is the breadth and length and height and depth, and to know the love of Christ that surpasses knowledge, that you may be filled with all the fullness of God" (Ephesians 3:17–19).

"There is no fear in love, but perfect love casts out fear" (1 John 4:18 ESV).

"And above all these put on love, which binds everything together in perfect harmony" (Colossians 3:14 ESV).

"Above all, keep loving one another earnestly, since love covers a multitude of sins" (1 Peter 4:8 ESV).

"Love is patient and kind; love does not envy or boast; it is not arrogant or rude. It does not insist on its own way; it is not irritable or resentful; it does not rejoice at wrongdoing, but rejoices with the truth. Love bears all things, believes all things, hopes all things, endures all things" (1 Corinthians 13:4–7 ESV).

"Serve one another humbly in love" (Galatians 5:13 ESV).

Chapter 8: The Leg of Fellowship

1　Excerpts from the 2018 AARP report on "Loneliness and Social Connections," by G. Oscar Anderson and Colette E. Thayer, PhD.

2   Excerpts from "Loneliness and risk of mortality: A longitudinal investigation in Alameda County, California," arch 2010, by Andrew C. Patterson and Gerry Veenstra.

3   Excerpts from *BMJ Journals, HEART*, on "Loneliness and social isolation as risk factors for coronary heart disease and stroke: systematic review and meta-analysis of longitudinal observational studies," June 10, 2016, vol. 102, no. 13, by Nicole K. Valtorta, Mona Kanaan, Simon Gilbody, Sara Ronzi, and Barbara Hanratty.

4   Excerpts from D. Perlman, L. A. Peplau (1981), "Towards a social psychology of loneliness, in Personal Relationships in Disorder," eds. S. Duck, R. Gilmour (London: Academic Press), 32–56.

5   Excerpts from the 2018 AARP report on "Loneliness and Social Connections," by G. Oscar Anderson and Colette E. Thayer, PhD.

6   Excerpts from "D. Perlman, L. A. Peplau (1981), "Towards a social psychology of loneliness, in Personal Relationships in Disorder," eds., S. Duck, R. Gilmour (London: Academic Press), 32–56.

7   Quote from "Song of the Phoenix," by Lily Fairchilde,1997, St. Martin's Press, NY.

8   "For the LORD's portion is his people, Jacob his allotted inheritance" (Deuteronomy 32:9).

9   "Do not be deceived: Bad company ruins good morals" (1 Corinthians 15:33).

10 "The person without the Spirit does not accept the things that come from the Spirit of God but considers them foolishness, and cannot understand them because they are discerned only through the Spirit" (1 Corinthians 2:14).

11 "Behold, how good and pleasant it is when brothers dwell in unity!" (Psalm 133:1).

"Iron sharpens iron, and one man sharpens another" (Proverbs 27:17 ESV).

"Two are better than one, because they have a good reward for their toil. For if they fall, one will lift up his fellow. But woe to him who is alone when he falls and has not another to lift him up! Again, if two lie together, they keep warm, but how can one keep warm alone? And though a man might prevail against one who is alone, two will withstand him—a threefold cord is not quickly broken" (Ecclesiastes 4:9–12 ESV).

12 "Bear one another's burdens, and so fulfill the law of Christ" (<u>Galatians 6:2</u> ESV).

"So then, as we have opportunity, let us do good to everyone, and especially to those who are of the household of faith" (<u>Galatians 6:10</u> ESV).

"So if there is any encouragement in Christ, any comfort from love, any participation in the Spirit, any affection and sympathy, complete my joy by being of the same mind, having the same love, being in full accord and of one mind. Do nothing from rivalry or conceit, but in humility count others more significant than yourselves. Let each of you look not only to his own interests, but also to the interests of others. Have this mind among yourselves, which is yours in Christ Jesus" (<u>Philippians 2:1–5</u> ESV).

13 "Finally, brothers, rejoice. Aim for restoration, comfort one another, agree with one another, live in peace; and the God of love and peace will be with you" (<u>2 Corinthians 13:11</u>).

"Do not judge, or you too will be judged. For in the same way you judge others, you will be judged, and with the measure you use, it will be measured to you. Why do you look at the speck of sawdust in your brother's eye and pay no attention to the plank in your own eye? How can you say to your brother, 'Let me take the speck out of your eye,' when all the time there is a plank in your own eye? You hypocrite, first take the plank out of your own eye, and then you will see clearly to remove the speck from your brother's eye" (Matthew 7:1–5 ESV).

14 "That they may all be one, just as you, Father, are in me, and I in you, that they also may be in us, so that the world may believe that you have sent me. The glory that you have given me I have given to them, that they may be one even as we are one, I in them and you in me, that they may become perfectly one, so that the world may know that you sent me and loved them even as you loved me" (<u>John 17:21–23</u> ESV).

"And all who believed were together and had all things in common. And they were selling their possessions and belongings and distributing the proceeds to all, as any had need. And day by day, attending the temple together and breaking bread in their homes, they received their food with glad and generous hearts, praising God and having favor with all the people. And the Lord added to their number day by day those who were being saved" (Acts 2:44–47 ESV).

"For just as the body is one and has many members, and all the members of the body, though many, are one body, so it is with Christ" (1 Corinthians 12:12 ESV).

"Now you are the body of Christ and individually members of it" (1 Corinthians 12:27 ESV).

"Let the word of Christ dwell in you richly, teaching and admonishing one another in all wisdom, singing psalms and hymns and spiritual songs, with thankfulness in your hearts to God" (Colossians 3:16 ESV).

"Therefore encourage one another and build one another up, just as you are doing" (1 Thessalonians 5:11 ESV).

Chapter 9: The Leg of the Faith Disciplines

1   "What good is it, my brothers and sisters, if someone claims to have faith but has no deeds? Can such faith save them? Suppose a brother or a sister is without clothes and daily food. If one of you says to them, 'Go in peace; keep warm and well fed,' but does nothing about their physical needs, what good is it? In the same way, faith by itself, if it is not accompanied by action, is dead. But someone will say, 'You have faith; I have deeds.' Show me your faith without deeds, and I will show you my faith by my deeds. You believe that there is one God. Good! Even the demons believe that—and shudder. You foolish person, do you want evidence that faith without deeds is useless? Was not our father Abraham considered righteous for what he did when he offered his son Isaac on the altar? You see that his faith and his actions were working together, and his faith was made complete by what he did. And the scripture was fulfilled that says, 'Abraham believed God, and it was credited to him as righteousness,' and he was called God's friend. You see that a person is considered righteous by what they do and not by faith alone. In the same way, was not even Rahab the prostitute considered righteous for what she did when she gave lodging to the spies and sent them off in a different direction? As the

body without the spirit is dead, so faith without deeds is dead" (James 2:14–26).

2   This quote has often been attributed to Dwight Moody but was originated by the British Revivalist Henry Varley as recorded in *Crucial Experiences in the Life of D.L. Moody, by* Paul Gericke, Insight Press, 1978.

3   Excerpt from *The Spirit of the Disciplines, Understanding How God Changes Lives,* by Dallas Willard, Harper San Francisco, 1991.

4   Excerpt from *Renovation of the Heart, Putting on the Character of Christ,* by Dallas Willard, Navigators, 2002.

5   Submit to one another out of reverence for Christ. Wives, submit yourselves to your own husbands as you do to the Lord. For the husband is the head of the wife as Christ is the head of the church, his body, of which he is the Savior. Now as the church submits to Christ, so also wives should submit to their husbands in everything. Husbands, love your wives, just as Christ loved the church and gave himself up for her to make her holy, cleansing her by the washing with water through the word, and to present her to himself as a radiant church, without stain or wrinkle or any other blemish, but holy and blameless. In this same way, husbands ought to love their wives as their own bodies. He who loves his wife loves himself. After all, no one ever hated their own body, but they feed and care for their body, just as Christ does the church, for we are members of his body. For this reason a man will leave his father and mother and be united to his wife, and the two will become one flesh. This is a profound mystery, but I am talking about Christ and the church. However, each one of you also must love his wife as he loves himself, and the wife must respect her husband" (Ephesians 5:21–33).

6   The 7 Habits of Highly Effective People, Steven Covey, Free Press, 1989.

7   Additional scriptures relative to the faith disciplines include:

"A man without self-control is like a city broken into and left without walls" (Proverbs 25:28).

"If you are willing and obedient, you shall eat the good of the land" (Isaiah 1:19).

"Do you not know that in a race all the runners run, but only one receives the prize? So run that you may obtain it. Every athlete exercises self-control in all things. They do it to receive a perishable wreath, but we an imperishable. So

I do not run aimlessly; I do not box as one beating the air. But I discipline my body and keep it under control, lest after preaching to others I myself should be disqualified" (1 Corinthians 9:24–27).

"For you were called to freedom, brothers. Only do not use your freedom as an opportunity for the flesh, but through love serve one another" (Galatians 5:13).

"What you have learned and received and heard and seen in me—practice these things, and the God of peace will be with you" (Philippians 4:9–13).

"That each one of you know how to control his own body in holiness and honor" (1 Thessalonians 4:4).

"For God gave us a spirit not of fear but of power and love and self-control" (2 Timothy 1:7).

"Do your best to present yourself to God as one approved, a worker who has no need to be ashamed, rightly handling the word of truth" (2 Timothy 2:15).

"For the moment all discipline seems painful rather than pleasant, but later it yields the peaceful fruit of righteousness to those who have been trained by it" (Hebrews 12:11).

"As obedient children, do not be conformed to the passions of your former ignorance" (1 Peter 1:14).

Chapter 10: The Stretcher of Being Spiritually Minded

1   Some excellent points on the importance of being spiritually minded and practicing it can be found in the following books:

How to Think: A Survival Guide for a World at Odds, Alan Jacobs, Crown Publishing, 2017.

Think: The Life of the Mind and the Love of God, John Piper, Crossway Publishers, 2010.

Breaking Bread with the Dead: A Reader's Guide to a More Tranquil Mind, Alan Jacobs, Penguin Random House 2020.

Get Out of Your Head: Stopping the Spiral of Toxic Thoughts, Jennie Allen, Right Now Media, 2020.

Practice the Presence of God, Brother Lawrence, originally published 1692, Reprint by Whittaker House, 1982.

2   See Acts 2:1–41.

3   "As soon as Jesus was baptized, He went up out of the water. Suddenly the heavens were opened, and He saw the Spirit of God descending like a dove and resting on Him. And a voice from heaven said, This is My beloved Son, in whom I am well pleased!" (Matthew 3:16–17).

"I am the way and the truth and the life. No one comes to the Father except through me" (John 14:6).

"For a child will be born to us, a son will be given to us; And the government will rest on His shoulders; And His name will be called Wonderful Counselor, Mighty God, Eternal Father, Prince of Peace" (Isaiah 9:6–7).

4   Excerpt from *Repent! The Forgotten Doctrine of Salvation, a sermon preached by Ray Pritchard,* president of Keep Believing Ministries, 10/06/2006, and can be found on their website, www.keepbelieving .com.

5   This statistic comes from a team of psychology experts at the Department of Psychology at Queen's University in Canada, led by Jordan Poppenk, and reported on in a 7/15/20 *Newsweek* article by Jason Murdock, "Humans Have More than 6,000 Thoughts per Day, Psychologists Discover."

6   "Have nothing to do with godless myths and old wives' tales; rather, train yourself to be godly" (1 Timothy 4:7).

"The thoughts of the righteous are just; the counsels of the wicked are deceitful" (Proverbs 12:5).

"The heart of the righteous ponders how to answer, but the mouth of the wicked pours out evil things" (Proverbs 15:28).

7   Other translations of this verse include:

"For you are not setting your mind on the things of God, but on the things of man" (ESV).

"You're not thinking God's thoughts, but human thoughts!" (ISV).

"For you are not setting your mind on God's interests, but man's [interests]" (NAS).

8   "For by grace you have been saved through faith. And this is not your own doing; it is the gift of God" (Ephesians 2:8).

9   See Luke 15:11–32.

"Let the wicked forsake his way, and the unrighteous man his thoughts; let him return to the LORD, that he may have compassion on him, and to our God, for he will abundantly pardon. For my thoughts are not your thoughts, neither are your ways my ways, declares the LORD" (Isaiah 55:7–8).

"Search me, O God, and know my heart! Try me and know my thoughts! And see if there be any grievous way in me, and lead me in the way everlasting! (Psalm 139:23–24).

"I the LORD search the heart and test the mind, to give every man according to his ways, according to the fruit of his deeds" (Jeremiah 17:10).

"Trust in the LORD with all your heart, and do not lean on your own understanding" (Proverbs 3:5).

10   Some other versions help us to see this point:

"Let God transform you into a new person by changing the way you think" (NLT).

"Do not conform yourselves to the standards of this world, but let God transform you inwardly by a complete change of your mind" (GNT).

"Don't become like the people of this world. Instead, change the way you think" (GWT).

"Don't become so well-adjusted to your culture that you fit into it without even thinking. Instead, fix your attention on God. You'll be changed from the inside out. Readily recognize what he wants from you, and quickly respond to it (Message).

11 "This day I call the heavens and the earth as witnesses against you that I have set before you life and death, blessings and curses. Now choose life, so that you and your children may live and that you may love the LORD your God, listen to his voice, and hold fast to him" (Deuteronomy 30:19–20).

"Now fear the LORD and serve him with all faithfulness. Throw away the gods your ancestors worshiped beyond the Euphrates River and in Egypt, and serve the LORD. But if serving the LORD seems undesirable to you, then choose for yourselves this day whom you will serve, whether the gods your ancestors served beyond the Euphrates, or the gods of the Amorites, in whose land you are living. But as for me and my household, we will serve the LORD" (Joshua 24:14–15).

Chapter 11: Building Five Habits for Being Spiritually Minded

1 "For the LORD your God goes with you; he will never leave you nor forsake you" (Deuteronomy 31:6).
2 "God didn't give us a cowardly spirit but a spirit of power, love, and good judgment" (2 Timothy 1:7 GWT).

"Peace I leave with you; my peace I give to you. Not as the world gives do I give to you. Let not your hearts be troubled, neither let them be afraid" (John 14:27).

"Do not be anxious about anything, but in everything by prayer and supplication with thanksgiving let your requests be made known to God. And the peace of God, which surpasses all understanding, will guard your hearts and your minds in Christ Jesus. Finally, brothers, whatever is true, whatever is honorable, whatever is just, whatever is pure, whatever is lovely, whatever is commendable, if there is any excellence, if there is anything worthy of praise, think about these things. What you have learned and received and heard and seen in me—practice these things, and the God of peace will be with you" (Philippians 4:6–9).

3   "Not that I have already obtained all this, or have already been made perfect, but I press on to take hold of that for which Christ Jesus took hold of me. Brothers, I do not consider myself yet to have taken hold of it. But one thing I do: Forgetting what is behind and straining toward what is ahead, I press on toward the goal to win the prize of God's heavenly calling in Christ Jesus" (Philippians 3:12–14).
4   Excerpt from *Rich Dad, Poor Dad*, by Robert Kiyosaki, Warner Book edition, 1997.
5   "For the word of God is living and active. Sharper than any double-edged sword, it pierces even to dividing soul and spirit, joints and marrow. It judges the thoughts and intentions of the heart" (Hebrews 4:12).

"The law of the LORD is perfect, reviving the soul; the testimony of the LORD is sure, making wise the simple" (Psalm 19:7).

"Behold, you delight in truth in the inward being, and you teach me wisdom in the secret heart" (Psalm 51:6).

6   *Every Man's Struggle*, Stephen Arterburn and Fred Stoker, Waterbrook Press, 2000.
7   "There was a man named Job, living in the land of Uz, who worshiped God and was faithful to him. He was a good man, careful not to do anything evil" (Job 1:1 GNT).
8   "Blessed is the one who does not walk in step with the wicked or stand in the way that sinners take or sit in the company of mockers, but whose delight is in the law of the LORD, and who meditates on his law day and night. That person is like a tree planted by streams of water, which yields its fruit in season and whose leaf does not wither—whatever they do prospers" (Psalm 1:1–3).

"May the words of my mouth and the meditation of my heart be pleasing in your sight, O Lord, my rock and my redeemer" (Psalm 19:30).

"You keep him in perfect peace whose mind is stayed on you, because he trusts in you" (Isaiah 26:3).

"Set your minds on things that are above, not on things that are on earth" (Colossians 3:2).

"Let the word of Christ dwell in you richly, teaching and admonishing one another in all wisdom, singing psalms and hymns and spiritual songs, with thankfulness in your hearts to God" (Colossians 3:16).

Chapter 12: Assembling Faith

1   "And God is able to make all grace abound to you, so that having all sufficiency in all things at all times, you may abound in every *good work*" (2 Corinthians 9:8 ESV).

"For as the body apart from the spirit is dead, so also faith apart from works is dead" (James 2:26 ESV).

"So then each of us will give an account of himself to God" (Romans 14:12 ESV).

"One who is faithful in a very little is also faithful in much, and one who is dishonest in a very little is also dishonest in much" (Luke 16:10 ESV).

"Go to the ant, O sluggard; consider her ways, and be wise" (Proverbs 6:6 ESV).

"For we must all appear before the judgment seat of Christ, so that each one may receive what is due for what he has done in the body, whether good or evil" (2 Corinthians 5:10 ESV).

2   Other versions translate verse 12:

"Work hard to show the results of your salvation, obeying God with deep reverence and fear" (NLT).

"Continue to work out your salvation [that is, cultivate it, bring it to full effect, actively pursue spiritual maturity] with awe-inspired fear and trembling [using serious caution and critical self-evaluation to avoid anything that might offend God or discredit the name of Christ]" (AMP).

"So work with fear and trembling to discover what it really means to be saved" (CEV).

"Continue working out your salvation with awe and reverence" (NET).

3   "No, in all these things we are more than conquerors through him who loved us. For I am convinced that neither death nor life, neither angels nor demons, neither the present nor the future, nor any powers, neither height nor depth, nor anything else in all creation, will be able to separate us from the love of God that is in Christ Jesus our Lord" (Romans 8:37–39).

4   "Greater love has no one than this, that someone lay down his life for his friends" (John 15:13 ESV).

"Judge not, that you be not judged. For with the judgment you pronounce you will be judged, and with the measure you use it will be measured to you. Why do you see the speck that is in your brother's eye, but do not notice the log that is in your own eye? Or how can you say to your brother, 'Let me take the speck out of your eye,' when there is the log in your own eye? You hypocrite, first take the log out of your own eye, and then you will see clearly to take the speck out of your brother's eye" (Matthew 7:1–5 ESV).

"In the same way, let your light shine before others, so that they may see your good works and give glory to your Father who is in heaven" (Matthew 5:16 ESV).

"Therefore, confess your sins to one another and pray for one another, that you may be healed. The prayer of a righteous person has great power as it is working" (James 5:16 ESV).

Chapter 13: Sharing Faith

1   This section in Matthew is known as the "Great Commission" to the church:

Then Jesus came to them and said, 'All authority in heaven and on earth has been given to me. Therefore go and make disciples of all nations, baptizing them in the name of the Father and of the Son and of the Holy Spirit, and teaching them to obey everything I have commanded you. And surely I am with you always, to the very end of the age'" (Matthew 28:18–20).

2   *How to Win Friends and Influence People,* Dale Carnegie, Simon and Shuster, 1936.

3   "But the Helper, the Holy Spirit, whom the Father will send in my name, he will teach you all things and bring to your remembrance all that I have said to you" (John 14:26 ESV).

"Likewise the Spirit helps us in our weakness. For we do not know what to pray for as we ought, but the Spirit himself intercedes for us with groanings too deep for words" (Romans 8:26 ESV).

"But you will receive power when the Holy Spirit has come upon you, and you will be my witnesses in Jerusalem and in all Judea and Samaria, and to the end of the earth" (Acts 1:8 ESV).

"And we impart this in words not taught by human wisdom but taught by the Spirit, interpreting spiritual truths to those who are spiritual" (1 Corinthians 2:13 ESV).

"He saved us, not because of works done by us in righteousness, but according to his own mercy, by the washing of regeneration and renewal of the Holy Spirit, whom he poured out on us richly through Jesus Christ our Savior" (Titus 3:5–6 ESV).

"For it is not you who speak, but the Spirit of your Father speaking through you" (Matthew 10:20 ESV).

4   "But Moses said, 'Pardon your servant, Lord. Please send someone else.' Then the LORD's anger burned against Moses and he said, 'What about your brother, Aaron the Levite? I know he can speak well. He is already on his way to meet you, and he will be glad to see you. You shall speak to him and put words in his mouth; I will help both of you speak and will teach you what to do. He will speak to the people for you, and it will

be as if he were your mouth and as if you were God to him'" (Exodus 4:13–16).

5   "I am the way and the truth and the life. No one comes to the Father except through me. If you really know me, you will know my Father as well. From now on, you do know him and have seen him" (John 14:6 NIV).

"He is the image of the invisible God, the firstborn of all creation. For by him all things were created, in heaven and on earth, visible and invisible, whether thrones or dominions or rulers or authorities—all things were created through him and for him. And he is before all things, and in him all things hold together" (Colossians 1:15–17 (ESV).

"For God so loved the world, that he gave his only Son, that whoever believes in him should not perish but have eternal life. For God did not send his Son into the world to condemn the world, but in order that the world might be saved through him" (John 3:16–17 ESV).

6   "For we do not wrestle against flesh and blood, but against the rulers, against the authorities, against the cosmic powers over this present darkness, against the spiritual forces of evil in the heavenly places" (Ephesians 6:12 ESV).

"For everyone who has been born of God overcomes the world. And this is the victory that has overcome the world, our faith. Who is it that overcomes the world except the one who believes that Jesus is the Son of God? (1 John 5:4–5 ESV).

"For the weapons of our warfare are not of the flesh but have divine power to destroy strongholds" (2 Corinthians 10:4 ESV).

7   "But in your hearts revere Christ as Lord. Always be prepared to give an answer to everyone who asks you to give the reason for the hope that you have. But do this with gentleness and respect" (1 Peter 3:15).

Chapter 14: The Hope Set Before Us

1 "For whatever was written in former days was written for our instruction, that through endurance and through the encouragement of the Scriptures we might have hope" (Romans 15:4 ESV).

"I wait for the LORD, my soul waits, and in his word I hope" (Psalm 130:5 ESV).

"O Israel, hope in the LORD! For with the LORD there is steadfast love, and with him is plentiful redemption" (Psalm 130:7 ESV).

2 The entire section reads:

"The next day John saw Jesus coming toward him and said, 'Look, the Lamb of God, who takes away the sin of the world! This is the one I meant when I said, a man who comes after me has surpassed me because he was before me. I myself did not know him, but the reason I came baptizing with water was that he might be revealed to Israel.' Then John gave this testimony: 'I saw the Spirit come down from heaven as a dove and remain on him. And I myself did not know him, but the one who sent me to baptize with water told me, The man on whom you see the Spirit come down and remain is the one who will baptize with the Holy Spirit. I have seen and I testify that this is God's Chosen One'" (John 1:29–33).

3 "We have this as a sure and steadfast anchor of the soul, a hope that enters into the inner place behind the curtain" (Hebrews 6:19 ESV).

"Waiting for our blessed hope, the appearing of the glory of our great God and Savior Jesus Christ" (Titus 2:13 ESV).

"Because of the hope laid up for you in heaven. Of this you have heard before in the word of the truth, the gospel" (Colossians 1:5 ESV).

4 "Rejoice in hope, be patient in tribulation, be constant in prayer" (Romans 12:12 ESV).

"But they who wait for the Lord shall renew their strength; they shall mount up with wings like eagles; they shall run and not be weary; they shall walk and not faint" (Isaiah 40:31 ESV).

"Through him we have also obtained access by faith into this grace in which we stand, and we rejoice in hope of the glory of God. More than that, we rejoice in our sufferings, knowing that suffering produces endurance, and endurance produces character, and character produces hope, and hope does not put us to shame, because God's love has been poured into our hearts through the Holy Spirit who has been given to us" (Romans 5:2–5 ESV).

5   *It Is Well with My Soul*, written by Horatio Spafford in 1876.

Lyrics:

"When peace like a river, attendeth my way, When sorrows like sea billows roll; Whatever my lot, Thou hast taught me to know It is well, it is well, with my soul.

Though Satan should buffet, though trials should come, Let this blest assurance control, That Christ has regarded my helpless estate, And hath shed His own blood for my soul.

My sin, oh, the bliss of this glorious thought! My sin, not in part but the whole, Is nailed to the cross, and I bear it no more,
Praise the Lord, praise the Lord, O my soul!
For me, be it Christ, be it Christ hence to live: If Jordan above me shall roll,
No pang shall be mine, for in death as in life,
Thou wilt whisper Thy peace to my soul.
But Lord, 'tis for Thee, for Thy coming we wait, The sky, not the grave, is our goal; Oh, trump of the angel! Oh, voice of the Lord! Blessed hope, blessed rest of my soul.
And Lord, haste the day when the faith shall be sight, The clouds be rolled back as a scroll; The trump shall resound, and the Lord shall descend, A song in the night, oh my soul![c]
Refrain
It is well, (it is well), with my soul, (with my soul) It is well, it is well, with my soul."

6   "Blessed be the God and Father of our Lord Jesus Christ! According to his great mercy, he has caused us to be born again to a living hope through the resurrection of Jesus Christ from the dead" (1 Peter 1:3 ESV).

7   The entire section reads:

"But, as it is written, What no eye has seen, nor ear heard, nor the heart of man imagined, what God has prepared for those who love him, these things God has revealed to us through the Spirit. For the Spirit searches everything, even the depths of God. For who knows a person's thoughts except the spirit of that person, which is in him? So also no one comprehends the thoughts of God except the Spirit of God. Now we have received not the spirit of the world, but the Spirit who is from God, that we might understand the things freely given us by God. And we impart this in words not taught by human wisdom but taught by the Spirit, interpreting spiritual truths to those who are spiritual" (1 Corinthians 2:9–13).

8   Other versions translate the words "minds that are alert and fully sober" as:

"So prepare your minds for action and exercise self-control" (NLT).

"Be alert and think straight" (CEV).

"Therefore, prepare your minds for action, keep a clear head" (ISV).

"Therefore, your minds must be clear and ready for action" (GWT).

"So roll up your sleeves, put your mind in gear, be totally ready" (Message).

APPENDIX 4

RESOURCES FOR THE FAITH DISCIPLINES

The Spirit of the Disciplines, Understanding How God Changes Lives, Dallas Willard, Harper San Francisco, 1991.

Renovation of the Heart, Putting on the Character of Christ, Dallas Willard, Navigators, 2002.

Celebration of Discipline, Richard Foster and Kathryn A. Helmers, Harper New York, 1992

The Hole In Our Gospel, Richard Stearns, Thomas Nelson Nashville, 2009

Prayer in the Night, For Those Who Work or Watch or Weep, Tish Harrison Warren, InterVarsity Press Illinois, 2021

Get Out Of Your Head, Stopping the Spiral of Toxic Thoughts, Jennie Allen, Waterbrook Colorado Springs, 2020

An Introduction to Apologetics, Defending Your Faith, R. C. Sproul, Crossway, Illinois, 2003